By M
fror

War Diary of
Lieutenant Edward Sidney Hacker
Army Service Corps

August 4th to November 30th 1914

Editor
The Rt Revd George Hacker

Centenary Edition
Self published with Amazon CreateSpace 2015

Acknowledgements

The bulk of the research on the Diary was carried out in 2006 and resulted in the publication of a limited edition of around thirty copies. It was printed privately at home on the Editor's own computer, and then bound and finished by Reeds Ltd of Penrith. Most of those listed below belong to that period.

However some further research took place between 2006 and the preparation of a Centenary Edition of the Diary in 2014, especially in the area of E.S.H.'s life and career, and a number of people were of considerable help to the Editor in this. They too are listed below.

The Editor wishes to thank the following for their help and encouragement:

The Archivist at the Royal Logistic Corps Museum, Mr Gareth Mears, for the considerable research undertaken on the Editor's behalf, especially into E.S.H.'s later career, and also for permission to use the material in the Centenary Edition.

Lieut-Colonel Michael Young, for permission to use some of the photographs in his postcard collection.

The Archivist, Mr Stuart Eastwood, and Mr Tony Goddard at the King's Own Royal Border Regiment Museum (now Cumbria's Museum of Military Life) in Carlisle Castle for permission to research their Army Lists.

Captain Paul Hinkley Q.A.R.A.N.C., for loan of books and for the Dictionary of Great War Slang, compiled by himself.

The late Steve Mitchell for research undertaken on the Editor's behalf into the London Gazette at the Public Record Office.

The former Head of Archives and Local Studies at the Records Office, Shakespeare Birthplace Trust, Dr Robert Bearman, for material about Trinity College, Stratford-upon-Avon. Also the present Collections Archivist, Hazel Gatford, for permission to use an early photograph of the College.

The Imperial War Museum for permission to use two photographs from its photographic collection.

The Secretary and Editor of the Old Kelleian Club, Frances Alexander, for research into E.S.H.'s time at Newton College.

The Curatorial Officer, Admiralty Library, Naval Historical Branch, Ian MacKenzie, for information about the so-called 'Royal Naval School', Lee on Solent.

Shaun Hullis for introducing me to the self publishing programme Amazon CreateSpace.

Copyright © 2015 George Hacker
All rights reserved

Preface to the Centenary Edition

My father's War Diary was well received by members of the family, when I first published it in a very limited edition in 2006, and as the centenary of the events described in it approached, I began to wonder whether an attempt should be made to share its contents with a wider readership. Accordingly I approached a publishing house, which claimed to specialise in matters of military interest, but with no success. That was in September 2013 and the project remained on ice for nearly a year.

Then in August 2014 I had an unexpected break. A close friend of ours, Joan Gregg, rang to say that her late husband's long-awaited wartime memoirs were about to be published and would be available on Amazon. This was very good news as Colonel Tresham Gregg, who became a very special friend of mine after I married him and Joan in 1999 (he was 80 at the time!), had had a very adventurous war, escaping from a prison camp in 1943 to lead a group of Italian partisans, and with them liberating an entire valley from the Germans. When he died in March 2014, I was afraid that his memoirs would never be published.

I needn't have worried. Shaun Hullis, a former master at Winchester College, had done his research very thoroughly, staying with Tresham and Joan, and recording Tresham's memories of his life at considerable length. Like me, he failed to find a publisher, but, unlike me, knew of Amazon's self publishing programme, CreateSpace, and made use of that to produce the book. The result was 'Captains Courageous: Gunner Gregg , Donny Mackenzie, & the Liberation of the Nure Valley, 1944'. When I wrote to him, congratulating him on his achievement, I also asked about CreateSpace, and received a most helpful reply. The result is this book, and I shall always be grateful to Shaun for introducing me to the programme and encouraging me to try it.

This Centenary Edition varies very little from that of 2006. I have updated some of the biographical information (page 5) after further research into E.S.H.'s schooldays, and have updated one or two small details in other sections. The biggest change is in the Resources section on pages 113-115, where I have included a number of new books, and considerably expanded my assessments of the others. I hope readers will find this helpful.

Finally Shaun Hullis' decision to call Tresham Gregg by his army nickname 'Gunner' alerted me to the fact that I had never explained why I used my father's initials instead of his name in both editions of the Diary. The answer is that he too had several names—'Ted' (never 'Edward') within his family and to my mother, and most confusingly 'George' to his army friends. In the end I settled for the neutral 'E.S.H.'

George Hacker , January 2015

*Edward Sidney Hacker around the age of eighteen
from a portrait by his Uncle
Arthur Hacker R.A.*

Table of Contents

Acknowledgements	ii
Preface to the Centenary Edition	iii
Table of Contents	v
Editor's Introduction	1
Edward Sidney Hacker—*A Biographical Sketch*	5
THE WAR DIARY—*Text and Notes*	20
APPENDICES	
Appendix 1: Order of Battle—August 1914	82
Appendix 2: Order of Battle—November 1914	85
Appendix 3: Army Colleagues and Acquaintances	91
Appendix 4: Extracts from the Corps Journal	99
Appendix 5: 'Old Bill'	108
Appendix 6: E.S.H.'s Army Records—Relevant Entries	109
Appendix 7: Resources	113
INDEX OF MAPS	
Arrival in France and First Contact with the Enemy—Aug. 19-23	28
The Retreat from Mons 1—Aug. 23-30	34
The Retreat from Mons 2—Aug. 31 to Sept. 10	44
The Advance to the Aisne—Sept. 6-12 On the Aisne—Sept. 13 to Oct. 3	48
The Move to Flanders—Oct. 2-13	60
The Area around Ypres—Oct. 13 to Nov. 30	67

Editor's Introduction

My father's *War Diary*, written during the first few months of the First World War, sat on my bookshelf unopened for quite a few years. I remember glancing at it once, and deciding that it was rather dull, full of references to people that I had never heard of, and anyway, because of the writing, hardly worth the effort of deciphering.

How wrong I was! When I finally got round to reading it properly in the summer of 2003, I found it fascinating. Eye witness accounts are among the most precious of historical documents—and here was one of them, written in odd moments while momentous events unfolded all around. Fascinating too to glimpse these events through the eyes of a twenty-six year old from an upper class Edwardian family. In places it really is very typically English public school—particularly in the understated way in which he describes some of the horrors and dangers. On the other hand there are moments when the reality of war clearly gets home to him. This comes out especially when he talks about some of the civilians who were kind to him and his brother officers, and who gave them hospitality. My father had the advantage of speaking French fluently (he had been sent to live with a French family that spoke no English as part of his education), and this gave him a certain rapport with them and an insight into their fears and feelings as the Germans approached. On a lighter note, my wife's comment on reading the first few pages was: 'This is all about *food*!'. A slight exaggeration , but when I started to think about it—yes, that is what you would expect from a healthy twenty-six year old, caught up in a situation where you never quite knew where the next meal was coming from. And that in itself has its own fascination—not least for those who are interested in the way our eating habits have changed down the years!

Of course transcribing the *Diary* was not enough. I quickly found myself caught up in researching the background to it, and trying to relate some of the references in it to actual events. And that has proved to be a fascinating exercise as well. I thought I knew quite a bit about the First World War, but I soon discovered how ignorant I was, particularly about the war of movement during the Autumn of 1914. In many ways that is the most interesting period, when generals could still plot grand strategy over large areas of the map, when the professionalism and courage of the British infantry again and again saved the day, and when the cavalry, which my father was supplying, could still be used as cavalry in a reconnaissance screen often in advance of the main body of troops. Those first few months are interesting too in the way they show how utterly unprepared all of the combatants were for the kind of war which developed—the French going into battle in their *pantalons rouges* and the British with an army more suited to small colonial wars. Even the Germans underestimated the

~~Wednesday~~ Tuesday
August 4th 1914.
 Having ~~been~~ waited for nearly a week we received the order to Mobilize at 8.0P.M today. I was appointed as subaltern to the 5th Cavalry Brigade Ammunition Park so I at once reported to Capt. Goldsmith. I was given orders to proceed at 5.0A.M. tomorrow to Liverpool with an advanced party so I packed my kit & went to bed after having had some food.

Wednesday
~~Thursday~~ August 5th.
 This morning I was up at 5 a.m. & went up to the Mess to get the breakfast I had ordered, but the waiters were mobilized so I could only get a cup of tea & then picked up my party & went off in a hurry to
 about 10 miles away. We arrived in plenty of time for the train but were nearly left behind as the train was crowded & ~~getting~~ into what we thought were empty ~~extra~~ coaches but who proved to be another train. Our first change was Cheltenham where I left Godley's dog. From here I got a washing carriage & had a shave & to

deadliness of modern weapons in defence, which was to wreck their meticulously prepared plans. 'Our first battle is a heavy, an unheard of heavy defeat, and against the English, the English we laughed at.' So wrote one German officer after the Battle of Mons—just one of the many indications that this was to be a different kind of war from any that had gone before.

One feature of the *Diary* is of particular—possibly unique—interest. As I quickly discovered, there is a vast amount of literature about the First World War, and there are eye witness accounts in plenty. But most of the latter are concerned with events in the front line where the excitement and action were. There are very few eye witness accounts of what it was like to be involved in supply and transport, and virtually nothing on mechanical transport—a new feature altogether in warfare. So readers of the *Diary* with a mechanical bent will be delighted with the descriptions of how to mend cracked cylinders, cannibalize spare parts from 'duds', and all the other improvisations which today seem to belong to a different world. And of course for the reader with a historical interest, there is the more general light which the *Diary* throws on the whole matter of how mechanical transport was used in the early days of the War and its importance in keeping the supplies and ammunition flowing. All of this makes the *Diary* a rare, if not unique, document.

The *Diary* covers the period from August 4th to November 30th 1914, the period of my father's first tour of duty in France (he didn't return until 5th May 1915). As can be seen from the illustrations, it is written in pencil in an Army Correspondence Book. As well as the text of the *Diary*, the book contains a few pages of rough notes at the beginning, together with some shopping lists on old envelopes, two identical postcards of the Ville Romain in Melun, and an unfinished letter dated October 30th 1914 to a Mrs 'St Marr' (*name illegible*) thanking her for some shirts. This last is important in that it includes the name of his unit as *56 Company A.S.C., 2nd Cavalry Division Ammunition Park*. I have not included any of this material in the pages which follow. As far as the actual text of the *Diary* is concerned, I have reproduced it with only the minimum of editorial alterations (in spite of occasional cries of protest from my spell checker!). I have however included a good deal of background information (the material in italics in the boxes), as I felt this would be of interest to readers and would help relate the *Diary* to the major events which were taking place.

Finally I have to say that transcribing and researching the *Diary* has had the strange effect of bringing my father back to life. More than fifty years have passed since he died, but there is a sense in which I can hear him speaking from every page. I had not expected this, and I am truly grateful for it.

George Hacker
June 2006

Edward Sidney Hacker as a young officer. The date of this photograph is uncertain, but it must have been taken after 1911 (note A.S.C. badges) and before 1916 (no medal ribbons).

Edward Sidney Hacker
A Biographical Sketch

Edward Sidney Hacker was born on 10th November 1887 at Newton Abbot in Devon. His father was Sidney Hacker, a local solicitor, who became County Coroner for Devon (Totnes District) in 1882. Sidney Hacker was long remembered as the person who conducted the inquest into the Babbacombe murder case, which achieved notoriety through the fact that the trap on the scaffold refused to work in spite of three attempts by the hangman (the murderer's sentence was later commuted to penal servitude). E.S.H.'s mother was Leila Kendall, and he was their second son. Altogether there were six children— three sons, followed by three daughters. The other person of note in the family was Sidney's younger brother, Arthur Hacker RA, who was a well-known painter, principally of portraits, London street scenes and subjects (of which one of the most famous is *The Annunciation*). Many of his paintings are still with family members.

According to E.S.H.'s army records, he was educated at *Newton College*, the local public school, now part of *Kelly College*, Tavistock, and preserved as *Newton House*, and at *Trinity College*, Stratford-upon-Avon. In fact he was only at *Newton College* for around a year, leaving in the summer of 1900. My mother once told me that he was not happy there, and that the boys went in for stone fights! Whatever the reason, he moved to the *Royal Naval School*, Lee on the Solent, and was there for about two years. We have his letters to his mother for that period, and although they are not dated, the postmarks on the envelopes cover the period from September 1900 to June 1902. I have a vague memory of an aunt telling me that he did think of joining the navy at one point, but changed his mind. Clearly he felt it tactful to omit this fact, when asked about his education for his Army records! Incidentally the *Royal Naval School* was a private school with no links either with royalty or the navy, and was later made to change its name.

Towards the end of 1903 he transferred to *Trinity College*, Stratford-upon-Avon (we have a picture of him as a member of the cricket team there, dated for that year). This also was a private school, founded in 1872 by Dr J.D.Collis, who was Vicar of Stratford-upon-Avon from 1867 until his death in 1879. Dr Collis had been a pupil of Dr Arnold, the famous headmaster of Rugby, and was heavily influenced by his ideas. The school flourished in its early days, with 152 boys in its peak year 1876, but by the time E.S.H. went there numbers were down to less than 50. It had also changed its character and by 1904 had become known as the 'Army School' and was training boys exclusively for the Army. This would explain why E.S.H. transferred to it. This role as an Army 'Crammer' did not last long and the school closed in 1908. The original building on the corner of Church Street and Chestnut Walk is still standing, and is now divided into flats.

From Stratford E.S.H. went to the *Royal Military Academy* at Woolwich. This was founded in 1741 and was intended, in the words of its first charter, to produce 'good officers of Artillery and perfect Engineers'. Entrance was by competitive written examination, and the *Academy* aimed to provide a high level of scientific education, while at the same time ensuring that their officers had the same level of military training as those serving in the Line. *R.M.A Woolwich* was commonly known as 'The Shop' because the first building was a converted workshop of the *Woolwich Arsenal*, and the expression 'talking shop' derives from this. A second establishment for training officers was opened at Sandhurst in 1799 under the name of the *Royal Military College*. Students at both establishments were known as 'gentlemen cadets', and unlike modern officer cadets, who are technically private soldiers paid and clothed by the *Ministry of Defence*, gentlemen cadets were not subject to military law. Their parents paid tuition and boarding fees, just as if they were at school or university, and there were 'cadetships' (the equivalent of scholarships) for sons of serving or former officers. This had the effect of confining entry to both establishments almost entirely to public schoolboys, often from families with a military connection. Both establishments were closed at the start of the Second World War, and then merged and reopened as the *Royal Military Academy Sandhurst* in 1947.

E.S.H. was commissioned as a Second Lieutenant into the Duke of Edinburgh's Royal Artillery Militia on 12th April 1906. This was a unit of the Royal Garrison Artillery, whose standard weapon was the 60 pounder gun, introduced in 1904 following the experience of the Boer War (We have a postcard of some of these 'Long Toms' in an old photo book of E.S.H.). The Militia had a long history, and together with the Yeomanry Cavalry and the Volunteers provided a reserve for the Regular Army. By 1906, however, the Militia had largely become a recruiting depot for the Regular Army, and that would seem to be how E.S.H. viewed it. In a contemporary article he is described as 'an Army Candidate', and he was accepted by the Regular Army in 1908. This was the year when the Secretary of State for War, Richard Haldane, made his sweeping reforms. Amongst many changes, he reconstituted the Militia as the 'Special Reserve' with the function of supplying trained manpower to the Regular Army, the Yeomanry with a similar function for the Cavalry, and the Volunteers as the new 'Territorial Force'.

E.S.H. was commissioned as a Second Lieutenant into the South Wales Borderers on 27th May 1908. My mother once told me that he changed from the artillery to the infantry because he didn't like the noise of the guns at close quarters! The South Wales Borderers as the 24th of Foot had distinguished themselves in the Marlborough campaigns, but are perhaps best remembered for their part in the Anglo-Zulu War, when in January 1879 they first suffered the disastrous defeat and massacre at Isandhlwana and then redeemed themselves with the heroic defence of Rorke's Drift. E.S.H.'s army records state that he had had experience both of India and South Africa. The 1st Battalion was in Karachi and Hyderabad, India, from March 1905 to March 1909 and then in Quetta, returning to England in December 1910. E.S.H. joined them in India shortly after his commissioning. He then went on to Pretoria in South Africa with the 2nd Battalion, which went there in January 1911. E.S.H. was promoted Lieutenant on 1st April 1911.

E.S.H. transferred to the Army Service Corps on 2nd October 1911, reverting to the rank of Second Lieutenant. Years later, when he came to retire, he was described as 'one of the small but distinguished group of A.S.C. officers who . . foresaw the vast potentialities of M.T., and by their zeal and vision established a very high standard of mechanical efficiency in the Corps'. Others, who also shared that vision, had already realised that with mechanisation there would be a need for trained personnel to manage and operate this new form of transport. So several years before in 1907 a syllabus of instruction had been devised for new A.S.C. officers and for those transferring from other regiments or corps. The scheme included a basic course at the training establishment at Aldershot, from which a selected number went on to do a nine month mechanical transport course. From these a further selection was made of those with special mechanical ability, and they were sent as apprentices to certain engineering firms for a twelve to eighteen month course. E.S.H.'s training followed this pattern, starting with a period at the *School of Instruction* at Aldershot from October 1911 until July 1913. The *Junior Officers' Course* was in three stages, the second of which involved a posting to a unit for twelve months of practical training. E.S.H. stayed in Aldershot for this and joined a service company there from January 1912 until January 1913. Then having completed the third stage of this course, he was posted to the Curragh in Southern Ireland, which together with Woolwich, Bulford, Portsmouth, Devonport, Colchester and Cork were the main UK postings for A.S.C. personnel. In November of that year he was selected for the *Long M.T. Course*, and this undoubtedly set the pattern for his future. He returned to Aldershot for this, completing it in July 1914. He would almost certainly have gone on to do an apprenticeship with one of the engineering firms, but his further training was interrupted by the War, and it was not until his return from France in 1920 that he was able to undertake the *M.T. Course* at *Thorneycroft*. He was promoted Lieutenant again on 2nd October 1912.

During his time at Aldershot E.S.H. trained with or got to know many of the officers mentioned in the *Diary*, some of whom became lifelong friends and colleagues (*see Appendix 3*). He also played a full part in the sporting side of army life. He is mentioned in the *Corps Journals* of the period as playing with the A.S.C. team in the Army Hockey Tournament (*February and March 1912*) and in the A.S.C. Tennis Tournament (*August 1912*). This too set a pattern for the future, and later *Journals* show him as a keen participant in a wide variety of sports, with golf in particular continuing right through to retirement and beyond.

After a few days at Bulford in August 1914, he was mobilised and embarked for France. August 4th to November 30th 1914 is the period covered by the *Diary*. On 30th November 1914 he returned home and was promoted Temporary Captain on the same day. His army records give no indication as to where he was stationed during the next few months, but it is likely to have been with 133 M.T. Company A.S.C. (He went to France with them in the May, and there is also a photo of someone who looks very like him in the forefront of a military funeral of one of the Company, which took place in Wells in March 1915). 133 Company was formed on 11th January 1915 and was a new unit, so it is likely that E.S.H. was involved in their training, as he had indeed expected to be (*see page 75 of the Diary*), and Wells in Somerset was one of the places where a number of A.S.C. units were trained. This was a period of rapid expansion for the Army, fuelled by Lord Kitchener's powerful appeal for volunteers.

133 M.T. Company moved to France between 5th and 11th May 1915 and was designated 14th Divisional Supply Column, with E.S.H. as its commanding officer. It's lorries reached Rouen on the 10th and 11th of May, and the Column set off for Flanders on the 13th to await the arrival of the 14th (Light) Division. This was a division of Kitchener's New Army and it began to arrive on the 25th. Initially without equipment of any kind, the Division was judged to be ready to go to France by May 1915, although it's move to the fighting front was delayed by lack of rifle and artillery ammunition. 14th Divisional Supply Column meanwhile moved to Ebblingham on the 27th, and then early in June to Caestre, where it remained for some time before moving yet again.

The 14th Division was involved in the action at Hooge in the Ypres salient at the end of July 1915, when they were the first British unit to be at the receiving end of German flamethrowers. For the rest of the year the Division remained in Flanders, with the Supply Column carrying out the usual routine of loading from the railhead and delivering to refilling points close to the front line. Then in January 1916 an advanced railhead was put into operation and supplies were offloaded direct by Horse Transport. So for a short time the Column was more or less out of action with regard to supply work, until it followed the 14th Division to Picardy in February 1916. Meanwhile E.S.H. had been promoted Captain and Temporary Major in September 1915.

During 1916 E.S.H.'s unit made frequent moves as the railhead changed its location. In May the railhead was at Tincques on the St Pol to Arras road, in

Trinity College, Stratford-upon-Avon, in its later days, around the time when E.S.H. was a pupil there. (Image reproduced by permission of the Shakespeare Birthplace Trust.)

1903—E.S.H. as a member of the cricket team at Trinity College, Stratford-upon-Avon.

1907 (probably)—E.S.H. as a second lieutenant in the Duke of Edinburgh's Royal Artillery Militia. This photo was clearly taken in camp, probably on the Isle of Wight (there are other photos of the camp in the same photo album).

1910—E.S.H.'s room in the Officers' Mess in Quetta. Note the topis and other headgear on the left. The pictures are of particular interest—photos of family members or their portraits. His father is in the centre bottom (behind the alarm clock), and to the left of him is a photo of Arthur Hacker RA, which is now in the Editor's possession.

1911—E.S.H. in South Africa (probably—there is a picture of Table Mountain on the opposite page in the photo album). Note also the black mourning armband.

1913—E.S.H. on the Long M.T. Course at Aldershot. There were 18 Participants in the photo, some of whom are mentioned in the Diary.

1915—133 Company A.S.C. A military funeral in Wells in March of that year. The officer nearest the camera in front of the parade looks very like E.S.H. (Photo from Lt-Col. Michael Young's postcard collection, reproduced here with his kind permission).

1915—Lorries of 133 Company A.S.C. setting off from Wells, Somerset, where a number of A.S.C. companies were trained for service in France. (Photo from Lt-Col. Michael Young's postcard collection, reproduced here with his kind permission).

1927—E.S.H.'s marriage to Carla Lanyon on July 30 at Farnborough Parish Church

1930—Lorna Doone winning the Heavyweight Cup, RASC point-to-point, ridden by Major Arden (P.A.).

1931—E.S.H. at Bulford.

1938—Gibraltar Races. E.S.H. (in the bowler hat) acting as Starter, with the Editor (in school cap) as his assistant!

1938—E.S.H. in Gibraltar.   *1943—E.S.H. at Reigate.*

August at Albert and then Hangest, and in September back at Albert again. It would have been a time of considerable activity with the build up to the Battle of the Somme. The 14th Division itself took part in the latter stages of the Somme battles, at Delville Wood in July and August 1916 and at Flers-Courcelette in September. E.S.H.'s unit would have been closely involved with the Division, bringing supplies from the railhead to the refilling points. This was frequently an exhausting operation, as supplies often had to be moved by night to avoid artillery fire and attacks by hostile aircraft. At times it could be dangerous too, when the Germans strafed the supply roads. Casualties, fortunately, were few (one man killed and one wounded by a bomb in December 1915), but the conditions under which the men worked were nevertheless pretty stressful. E.S.H. played his full part in this, and was mentioned in dispatches on 30th April 1916 and awarded the Military Cross on 1st January 1917. M.C.'s awarded as part of the *New Year Honours List* were usually for 'meritorious service' rather than specific acts of gallantry and were not accompanied by a citation, so we have no official record as to why it was awarded. However my mother once told me that he was given it for riding a motor bike under fire. This would fit the situation at the time, with E.S.H. having frequently to lead convoys of lorries under threat from shells and bombs.

At the beginning of February 1917 E.S.H. was appointed O.C. 'R' Corps Supply Column. Then in March 1918 he was appointed O.C. H.Q. 'R' Corps M.T. Column. This was probably not a completely new unit, but a change of name reflecting the major re-organisation of mechanical transport which took place during the winter of 1917-18. Previously M.T. companies dealt with particular types of load—ammunition, general supplies etc. and were organised accordingly. Now they all carried whatever was needed in a given situation and had a common establishment with which they were allocated to divisions and corps. Many were also placed under more centralised control as reserve units, which could be used where and when they were needed, and it would seem that E.S.H. was in command of one of these units. This more flexible arrangement fully justified itself during the German spring offensive of 1918, when the railway system was severely disrupted, and again with the rapid advance of the Allied armies during the last few months of the War, when communications were stretched to the limit. After the Armistice E.S.H. remained on the Continent, and in March 1919 was attached to No 7 M.T. V.R.P. No 3 District. Then in March 1920 he was attached to H.Q. British Troops in France and Flanders as Deputy Assistant Director of Transport Forward District, and finally in August of that year was appointed O.C. R.A.S.C Forward District (note the title 'Royal' which was conferred on the A.S.C. in December 1918 by King George V in recognition of its valuable service during the War).

E.S.H. returned home in mid-October 1920, and within a few weeks was sent as an apprentice to the *Thorneycroft Works* at Basingstoke for the *Mechanical*

Transport Course which the firm ran for the Army. John Isaac Thorneycroft was one of the pioneers of the motor industry, with his first petrol engined truck appearing as early as 1904. The firm had close links with the military, their 1912 J type 3 ton lorry being specifically designed to qualify for the subsidy scheme. Motor engineering was very different in those days, even though Henry Ford had already started his mass production methods which were to be the pattern for the future. I can remember my father telling me how he had been put with an experienced fitter soon after his arrival at the Works, and that for the first few weeks he did nothing except learn how to file straight! While still on the course he reverted to his substantive rank of Captain in January 1921.

The course was interrupted for a couple of months in April 1921 by a national emergency. On the 12th April E.S.H. was sent to the Mechanical Transport Depot at Bulford on standby because of a threatened strike by the miners', railway and transport unions. The trouble began in the coal industry, where wartime controls on coal were due to be removed and in the current economic slump employers planned to take advantage of this by lowering wages and setting them locally rather than by national negotiation. The miners went on strike on March 31st and on April 3rd coal was rationed. The Government was so worried that it recalled navy, army and air reserves and appealed for all 'loyal citizens capable of bearing arms', aged between 18 and 40 to volunteer for 90 days service in new units of the Regular Army, which would be called 'Defence Units'. The other two unions of the 'Triple Alliance' were due to start their strike on April 15th, but at the last minute decided not to come out in support of the *Miners' Federation*. This left the miners in a much weaker position, and after some negotiation and the Government agreeing to subsidise the coal industry, the strike ended on July 4th 1921. Meanwhile E.S.H. had resumed his Course at *Thorneycroft* in the latter half of June, and emerged with an A.M.I.Mech.E in November 1922.

The 1920's saw him with various postings in the South of England. He was appointed O.C. 12 M.T. Company stationed at Woolwich in November 1922, and then shortly afterwards at the end of April 1923 was sent to 'P' Company in Aldershot as an instructor under the Chief Inspector of Mechanical Transport. 'P' Company's task was to train officers and N.C.O.s from the R.A.S.C. and other arms in mechanical transport, and Aldershot was an exciting place to be at that time if you had a mechanical bent. It was a key centre not only for training, but for the design and testing of experimental vehicles. The twenties were a time of rapid mechanisation in the Army, hastened by the development of vehicles with a good cross country performance that could replace the horse (a 30 cwt truck as early as 1922 and a 3 ton 6-wheeled lorry by 1926—both with pneumatic tyres, which greatly improved their off road capability). By the beginning of 1923, twenty-three horse transport companies had been either amalgamated or disbanded, and by 1924 there were only eight R.A.S.C. horse transport units left. The final coup de grâce came in 1929, with the disbanding of all horse transport companies except for the Training Company in Aldershot.

In October 1927 E.S.H. was appointed O.C. 9 M.T. Company at Aldershot, and shortly afterwards in March 1928 O.C. 36 M.T. Company at Bulford. However the biggest change in his life came on 30th July 1927 when he married Carla Lanyon, a twenty-one year old living in Farnborough. My mother was in many ways very different from my father—artistic, widely read, later to become a gifted poet and writer—but they complemented each other well and it was a very happy marriage. She must have seemed incredibly modern to her Devon in-laws, with her clothes and make-up and independent outlook, and there are a few good stories about their initial contacts! She even had her own car—her father, who died in an accident before she was born, had left her a substantial sum of money in trust, so she was independent financially too.

E.S.H. was promoted Major in January 1929 and three years later at the beginning of 1932 moved to Salisbury, where he was made Deputy Assistant Director of Supplies and Transport Southern Command. During his time at Bulford he did not neglect his own training and completed the two *War Courses* (*Summer and Winter*) at Aldershot in 1931. At that time these provided the only opportunity, outside the *Staff College*, for studying the administrative and logistic problems of war in a realistic manner, and were always of great interest and value to those selected to take part.

E.S.H. also kept up his sporting activities whilst at Bulford and Salisbury, with golf in particular playing an important part in his life (*see Appendix 4*). This was the time too when he took part in a number of points-to-point (and broke his arm in the process!). His mare, Lorna Doone, twice won the Heavy-weight Cup in 1928 and 1930, though on these occasions not ridden by him, and he remained a keen supporter of the point-to-point throughout his life.

E.S.H. was four years in Salisbury—the longest time that he and my mother had had in one place since their marriage. To me it seemed as if we had never lived anywhere else, and it was a considerable shock when at the age of six I was told that we were moving to Kent. In fact it was only to be a short posting. E.S.H. took up his new appointment as O.C. R.A.S.C. Chatham in January 1936 and relinquished it a year later to become O.C. R.A.S.C. in Gibraltar. Meanwhile in March 1936 he was promoted Lieutenant-Colonel, having completed a *Senior Officers Course* at the School in Sheerness in 1935.

Gibraltar was a posting which carried considerable responsibility with it. It was in a key position strategically, guarding the entrance to the Mediterranean, and also where the action was at that time with Spain embroiled in a civil war. And the storm clouds were already building up for a much greater conflict. I remember my mother telling me how at the time of the Munich crisis in September 1938 one of the German pocket battleships was moored in Gibraltar harbour close to one of ours, and how the sailors from both ships joked with each other about the size of their guns! Socially it was an important posting too. There were dinners at Government House (including one at which the exiled Emperor of Ethiopia, Haile Selasse, was present), and my parents were expected to take their share in entertaining as well. And there were those other duties which inevitably come your way if you are a prominent person in a small community. My father was Chairman of the *Gibraltar Museum* and Secretary to the local branch of S.S.A.F.A., and my mother was Secretary to the *Gibraltar Girl Guides*. (*see Appendix 4*). But it was not all work. There was hunting in Spain with the *Royal Calpe Hunt*, and races organised by the *Yacht Club* (in *Lassie* with me aged eight as an extra crew member, competing with the Brigadier's boat with Captain Bond as crew—the latter a lifelong friend who was later to become Inspector R.A.S.C.). And there were early morning rides for the two of us, ending with a swim at the *Yacht Club*. As already mentioned my father was a keen horseman, and in Gibraltar put his point-to-point experience into practice by acting as Starter at the races for the *Gibraltar Jockey Club* (there was no airfield in those days). In many ways it was army life at its best—for all of us.

E.S.H. returned to England in June 1939, just a few months before the outbreak of World War II. He was promoted Colonel at the beginning of July and made Chief Inspector of Supplementary Transport. This was a key post with responsibility for the inspection of vehicles purchased under an impressment scheme, which had been worked out before the War. Mobilisation took place on September 1st, and soon after vehicles began to arrive at four collecting points, where they had to be received, registered, inspected, equipped and repainted. Speed was at a premium (so much so that a visiting officer to one of the Centres found that his car had been sprayed by mistake while he was at lunch!).

This task completed E.S.H. was selected for appointment as Assistant Inspector R.A.S.C. and given the duty rank of Brigadier. This was in May 1940, just before Dunkirk, and the following months were very hectic indeed. The B.E.F. had lost almost all its vehicles in France, and new units had to be formed and new equipment found as quickly as possible. It was a time of rapid expansion, and all these units had to be inspected and passed as fit for action. It was E.S.H.'s responsibility to carry this out, which he did usually about a month before each unit completed mobilisation. He then reported on its readiness for its war role, and backward units were given intensive training to bring them up to scratch. As the *Corps Journal* commentated on his retirement: 'The efficiency and outstanding achievements of R.A.S.C. units in all theatres are a tribute to the Assistant Inspector's pioneering work'.

An additional burden during this time was the absence of his wife and children. When invasion threatened my mother made the decision to take us all to Canada, knowing that the Nazis were not above using threats to family members to extract information. It was a risky business, and the return journey in January 1942 (from Bermuda, where we had moved three months earlier) was even riskier with the U boats hunting in packs. But we made it safely, and after that my parents were together again and we had something like a normal life—though the village near Dorking where we lived got bombed one night, and later was right in the path of the 'doodle bugs'. My father meanwhile in September 1942 had been appointed Deputy Director of Supplies and Transport South Eastern Command, and was conveniently based in Reigate, under ten miles from our home.

E.S.H. retired on 7th September 1943, but in December of that year returned to the active list as a Lieutenant-Colonel as O.C. R.A.S.C. Aldershot District. He finally retired with the rank of Brigadier on 26th February 1945. That however was not the end of his work for the nation. He was speedily enlisted by the *War Graves Commission* and given the job of providing the cemeteries in Europe with up to date equipment and transport, something which he was very well qualified to do. That was also not without its adventures as it involved a good deal of travelling, which had its own hazards in the immediate post-war period (he was once turned off the train onto an Italian frontier station in the middle of the night because his papers were not in order). The job with the *War Graves Commission* was of course a one off one, and as soon as the war cemeteries were properly equipped, he was able to retire fully

In retirement he kept up his links with the 'Corps'—he and my mother lived only a few miles from Aldershot, so were within easy reach of Buller Barracks and the Officers' Club. In those days, even with national service, the R.A.S.C. was like a big family. When researching the *Diary* I looked through the list of junior officers in *Hart's Army List* for 1915 and was amazed at the number that I knew—officers who were to be his colleagues for the whole of his career. And his subordinates always had the greatest affection for him—he was not the kind of officer who sought his own promotion at the expense of those under him. I can remember how warmly he was greeted, when he took me into Buller Officers' Mess shortly after I had been commissioned (also into the R.A.S.C. but National Service). In particular Corps Week was always a very special event for my parents, with a service in St George's Church, Aldershot (the Corps Church), and the associated events which provided an opportunity to meet many old friends. And my father kept up his sporting activities with the Corps as well. There are accounts in the *Corps Journal* of his taking part in the Golf Tournament between retired officers and serving officers, both in 1951 and 1952. Sadly all this came to an end, when in October 1953 he had a severe stroke . Though severely handicapped he battled on with great courage (he taught himself to type when he could no longer write) and was always cheerful and positive about his condition. He died on 18th September 1955 following another stroke and was given a military funeral at St George's Church. His name is included in the memorial list in the side chapel there.

George Hacker

E.S.H. at the height of his career in 1940. This photo was almost certainly taken for my mother in Canada, when we were all evacuated there in July 1940 (A letter from her to E.S.H. in early September says: 'The photographs have arrived, and the ones of you grace the wall of my sitting room proudly. I like the ones in a hat best'). I seem to remember we all had our photos taken in Harrods before we caught the train to Glasgow, from where we caught the boat to Canada.

The War Diary

Tuesday August 4th 1914

Having waited for nearly a week we received the order to mobilize at 6.0 p.m. today. I was appointed as subaltern to the 5th Cavalry Brigade Ammunition Park so I at once reported to Capt Goldsmith. I was given orders to proceed at 5.0 a.m. tomorrow to Liverpool with an advanced party, so I packed my kit and went to bed after having had some food.

Wednesday August 5th

This morning I was up at 5.0 a.m. and went up to the Mess to get the breakfast I had ordered, but the waiters were mobilized, so I could only get a cup of tea, and then picked up my party and went off in a hurry to a station about 10 miles away. We arrived in plenty of time for the train, but were nearly left behind as the train was crowded, and we got into what we thought were empty extra coaches, but which proved to be another train. Our first change was Cheltenham where I left Godley's dog. From here I got a washing carriage and had a shave and wash. We changed again at Worcester and then had an hour's wait at Birmingham, where I had a cup of tea and two ham sandwiches for breakfast at 12 noon. From here we caught a train at 1.30 p.m. and changed at Stafford and Crewe and then eventually reached Lime Street, Liverpool.

We had to march across Liverpool to the Exchange station and took a train to Seaforth, and then had to walk one and a quarter miles to our camp. We arrived in camp at 4.30 p.m., having had no food, and then had to go down to the station to draw our tents, blankets, camp equipment etc, and did not get our camp up until after dark. Martin was there with another advanced party and we went down to look for food, but there was no hotel or restaurant. We looked about and found a beer-house 'the Seaforth Arms', and they took pity on us and gave us some food in their private part of the pub and offered to let us feed there while we were in Seaforth. They are a man and his wife who are very nice, the wife being Devonshire and exactly like Connie Edis. They are called Burnett.

Thursday August 6th

This morning I was up at 6.0 a.m. and we got the camp put up and made everything ready for the arrival of the Company.

Lorries from all parts of the country arrived, and as the camping ground was too soft for them, they had to be left in the streets. Recruits and reservists came in thousands and there were more than we could cope with, and there

Supply and Transport

The Motor Transport Companies called **Ammunition Parks** carried both artillery and small arms ammunition as required. 5th Cavalry Brigade Ammunition Park was made up of men and vehicles from 56 M.T. Company A.S.C. and was responsible for supplying ammunition for the 13 pounder guns of J Battery Royal Horse Artillery (R.H.A.) which was attached to 5th Cavalry Brigade. The fundamental principle involved was that troops in action should never have to go back for ammunition. In a fluid situation this quite often meant operating in front of the main body of troops as can be seen from the earlier pages of the Diary. Later, in Flanders, when the front settled down and the situation became more static, Ammunition Parks were the link between the railhead and the refilling points close behind the front line.

In 1914 the war establishment of different units varied according to their purpose. One authority (April 1915) gives the establishment for a **Divisional Ammunition Park** as 5 officers (plus 1 attached from the Artillery) and 345 other ranks, looking after 65 3 ton lorries plus 6 for workshops and stores along with 4 cars and 9 motor cycles. It would appear from the Diary, however, that 56 M.T. Company was very far from being up to strength in August 1914. Apart from the gunner, Captain Hay, E.S.H. and Captain Goldsmith seem to have been the only officers at that point—but then one would have expected the unit to be under strength if it was only servicing a brigade. By October 1914, when 2nd Lieutenant Anderson arrived, 56 Company had become the Ammunition Park for the whole of the artillery in the newly formed 2nd Cavalry Division, and at that point was clearly moving towards its full establishment.

Supplies other than ammunition were carried from the railhead to the delivery points by **Divisional Supply Columns**. These were also M.T. companies of the A.S.C., and replaced the old horse transport columns for this link in the chain of supply. The change was made in the years preceding World War I and tried out in the manoeuvres of 1912. 5th Cavalry Brigade had its own Supply Column (46 M.T. Company A.S.C.).

Beyond the delivery points, each division had its own transport known as the **Divisional Train**, providing the main supply line to the Brigades and Battalions. The Divisional Train was made up of a headquarters and 4 horse transport (H.T.) companies, one for each brigade and one for divisional HQ. The Train moved with the Division and was under its command.

The terminology can be confusing, especially as the word 'column' is used somewhat loosely in the Diary, sometimes referring to a specific supply Column (e.g. page 31) and sometimes simply meaning a convoy of lorries or other vehicles (page 27). Also the two parts of the Divisional Train seem sometimes to have been referred to as the Ammunition Column (page 31) and Supply Column.

were no arrangements for feeding or sheltering them.

Yesterday all the big railway stations were crowded with reservists going off to rejoin their regiments and there were some heart-rending scenes on the platforms.

Goldsmith and the Company arrived at about 9.0 p.m. and I had some hot dinners ready for the men.

Mobilisation

Mobilisation, planned in very thorough detail and practised beforehand, was completed with smooth efficiency. The plans were extraordinarily detailed, and had been drawn up well before the War by Henry Wilson, Director of Military Operations at the War Office. On August 5th Commanding Officers were given 'Top Secret' files detailing the exact movements of their units with a precise timetable. It should be noted that, while the British Expeditionary Force of 1914 is always referred to as the 'Regular Army', in fact it was the Reservists who made up the greater part of its fighting strength. The units of the Home Army in peace time were generally below strength and full of recent recruits and young soldiers who were only partially trained. All these had to be left behind and the ranks filled with Reservists, who made up the greater fighting strength of the Army—sixty per cent of the B.E.F. One consequence of this was that many of the soldiers who went to war, while fully trained, were by no means physically fully fit, a fact to be borne in mind when the demands made on them during the retreat from Mons are considered.

August 9th to 15th

For the rest of the time we were at Seaforth we were taking on our vehicles, testing them, doing small repairs, getting our drivers, generally getting ready, and we were quite ready to embark by Monday 10th August. Goldsmith's fiancée, Miss Allen and her mother came to see him every day and once or twice they had tea in our tent, and another day I went into the Adelphi Hotel, Liverpool, and lunched with them. We were continually in Liverpool buying tyres, spares, etc. On the 13th I had to go down to the docks to load traction engines and trucks on the *Cornish City*, which was rather a slow job as they are heavy things to push about in the holds; but I kept steam up and drove mine into position. We lived with the Burnetts, who did us very well and were most kind. Mr Burnett's son enlisted in the A.S.C. as a driver. *Aquitania* is guarding the harbour.

> ## Motorised Transport
>
> *In 1911 the British started a modest programme with a scheme encouraging motor manufacturers to provide 'subsidy trucks'. In return for keeping trucks available for military use, manufacturers received an enrolment fee of £30 and a further £80 in six half-yearly instalments (1914 figures) for 3 ton and 30 cwt vehicles. The vehicles concerned had to meet rigid specifications laid down by the War Office, including a degree of standardisation. This made maintenance easier by reducing the number of spare parts required. The owners of the vehicles had to agree to maintain them in good working order and to surrender them for a fixed sum in time of national emergency.*
>
> *The subsidy scheme had a major effect on vehicle design generally, raising the standard considerably. It benefited business also, encouraging firms to buy vehicles, who normally would not have been able to afford them. And of course it allowed the army to build up a fleet of motor transport within the strictures of peace time budgets.*
>
> *By 1914 the War Office had only eighty vehicles of its own. The rest of the fleet, amounting by this time to nearly 1,200 in all, were 'subsidy' vehicles made by a select group of manufacturers, including Dennis, Maudslay, Hallford, Halley, Karrier, Leyland, Thorneycroft and Wolseley. These however were readily available and the B.E.F. was able to go to France equipped with 950 lorries and 250 motor cars.*

Sunday August 16th

This morning we were up early and took all our lorries down to the docks and embarked them on the *Withernsea*. Gross was embarkation officer and I had a chat with him. He is in the 24th Regiment. I embarked on the *Cragosworld* at 1.0 p.m. in charge of 150 men and 25 lorries, as there was no officer for it; and we sailed at 1.30 amidst much hooting etc.

Captain Collie was Master of the ship, assisted by the crew and Second Mate. They were very nice and let me have the run of the ship, and I lived with the Skipper and Mate. We had a very pleasant voyage, perfectly calm, and I spent most of my time on the bridge. During the whole voyage we were continually sighting French and English warships and torpedo boats, which would rush up to us to see who we were. We dropped anchor at 'Le Haver', as the crew called it, at 2.0 a.m.

Wednesday August 19th

We took a pilot on board and moved off at 5.0 a.m. up the Seine to Rouen. It was lovely going up the river and some of the prettiest scenery I have ever seen. The banks were crowded with French nearly all the way up, who were most enthusiastic and gave us a very hearty welcome, but they were mostly women and children and very few men.

We arrived at Rouen at 4.0 p.m., and I at once started off-loading the lorries, and got the last one off at 8.0 p.m. The French stevedores were very bad and constantly I had to re-sling lorries, which made things slow. They do much more talking than actual work and there never seems to be any foreman or responsible person.

I handed the lorries and men over to Noverre, and then went over to the *Withernsea* and reported to Goldsmith. I said au revoir to my skipper and took away my kit, and slept that night on the chart-room floor of the *Withernsea*.

Thursday August 20th

We took the lorries across the river and loaded them with ammunition at 6.30 a.m., after which I went down to test some French lubrication oil, as they wanted to issue us with steam engine oil. At about 11.0 a.m. I met Captain Hay, a gunner, who is in charge of our ammunition, who with Goldsmith and me had lunch at the Hôtel d'Angleterre, which was very expensive. This afternoon Goldsmith and I went out to see the Amiens road and the Vauxhall managed to do 50 mph. I came back and had tea at a small shop.

We were kept hanging about for a long time tonight for orders and then had to bring the Park over the river, so we did not get dinner till 9.0 p.m. at a very nice quiet hotel. Rouen closes at 8.0 p.m. so we had some difficulty in getting in. At 9.0 we walked up to the Rue d'Ernement where we were billeted, he at 80 and I at 78.

They were both very comfortable and they did us both very well, my host M. Journess giving me a tea and boiled egg breakfast at 5.0 a.m. He was a very decent fellow and spoke good English.

Friday August 21st

After my breakfast I waited for the car and suddenly Goldsmith's landlady came in and asked me to go over as Goldsmith can't talk French and he wanted to say something. When I got there all he wanted to know was the name of 'milk' in French.

We went down to the Company and picked up Hay and the interpreter and moved off for Amiens at 7.0. a.m. The interpreter is called Marcel Paulimier and lives at 25 Boulevard J'Eanne D'Arc, Rouen, and seems a good sort. We had a very long steep hill out of Rouen which made one or two of our radiators boil.

Motor Transport requisitioned by the British Army. A lorry once belonging to the Anglo-American Oil Company is unloaded from a transport ship at the quayside at Rouen in 1914. One can see why E.S.H. was so concerned that the lorries were slung properly, especially with a crowd of interested spectators watching nearby.

[Image no. HU 72008 ©IWM from the photographic archive of the Imperial War Museum, reproduced here under licence and with their kind permission.]

Motor lorries in Bac Saint-Maur, November 1914. These are typical of the sort of vehicles that E.S.H. would have had in his M.T. company. Note the solid tyres and lack of any protective windscreen. Not the most comfortable of vehicles to drive on the French pavé and in wet or snowy conditions

[Image no. Q 57364 ©IWM from the photographic archive of the Imperial War Museum, reproduced here under licence and with their kind permission.]

Before we had gone far the big end of one of our Halleys ran out and we tried to repair it, but could not, and it had to come on empty on three cylinders. The tyre of another Halley stripped, and I and two drivers spent an hour changing the wheel off a dud, and then found they would not fit; but we got a radiator and some useful spares. We arrived at Amiens (70 miles) at 5.0 p.m. The Halley without a tyre collapsed nine miles out of Amiens. Here a

Types of Vehicle

Three manufacturers of vehicles are mentioned on this page and on the one opposite.

Halley

Halley Industrial Motors Ltd was a Glasgow firm and was formed in 1901. Starting with steam wagons, in 1906 it moved over to petrol engined trucks, and during the period up to the War it had a range from 1½ to 6 tons. During the War Halley built some 400 3 ton subsidy lorries.

Thorneycroft

One of the pioneers of the motor industry, John Isaac Thorneycroft built his first steam van in 1896 at his Chiswick boatyard. The firm's association with the military began when in 1899 it supplied steam lorries to the army for use in the Boer War. Its first petrol engined truck, a 4 tonner, appeared in 1902. Encouraged by the Government's Subsidy Scheme, the firm produced the J type 3 tonner in 1912. This had a capacity of 3.4 tons, and a top speed of 14.5 m.p.h.. Unlike the chain drive systems traditionally used by Thorneycroft, the power in the J type was transmitted as an in-line arrangement via a four-speed gearbox and propeller shaft to a worm-driven live back axle. When WW1 broke out in August 1914, the War Office instructed Thorneycroft to prepare its entire output for military use. By the end of the war the firm had supplied about 5,000 J types in a number of body styles, including a flat bed lorry with a canvas cover, a box body that could open out into a mobile workshop and even as a carrier for an AA gun.

Wolseley

Based in Birmingham, Wolseley was Britain's largest car manufacturer, and initially contracted to provide cars for staff officers, and ambulances. However the Government had other ideas for the use of their plant, and by the end of the war the firm had produced a wide range products from aero engines to naval gun mountings. Amongst all these different items, Wolseley also built some 3,600 cars and lorries for the War Office, including both 30 cwt and 3 ton subsidy trucks.

petrol lorry of 5 D.A.P. [*Divisional Ammunition Park*] caught fire and set an 18 pounder ammunition lorry ablaze. Goldsmith showed great presence of mind by rushing to the lorry and throwing off the ammunition before it exploded, although some boxes were charred right through and it was a very near thing; but luckily no explosion occurred. There was great panic among the French, and they brought up a fire engine and put out the surrounding houses.

---

18 Pounder Ammunition

This would have been for units of the Royal Field Artillery, one of whose standard weapons was the 18 pounder field gun. The shell fired by this gun was 3.3 inch calibre (84mm) and weighed 18.5 lb (8.4kg). It had a maximum range of 6,525 yards (5.96km), with this distance being covered in a little over 12 seconds. It was the main field artillery weapon for the infantry as opposed to the 13 pounder used by the Royal Horse Artillery for the cavalry. This particular lorry would have belonged to 49 MT Company A.S.C. which was the Divisional Ammunition Park for the 5th Division.

In the mean time I had got our lorries well out of the way and then had to re-collect them. I then went off to fetch two lorries to replace the two Halleys which had broken down. At 10.0 p.m. I went off and had some food. I met Bearne here and did not know that he was in the A.S.C. till now. We had billets allotted us but slept in the car.

Saturday August 22nd

At 12.30 a.m. I had to take a lorry off three miles to draw petrol and rations, so did not get back to the car to sleep until 2.0 a.m. At 5.0 a.m. we got up and had some tea and bacon and biscuits, and moved off at 8.0 a.m., having replaced a leaking radiator for the one we picked up yesterday. The Halley on which we placed it was knocking badly, so we let it run empty and slowly.

One of our lorries (a Thorney) over-heated at the brake and caught fire. Another (a Wolseley) got its oil feed choked. But they caught up again. We broke a petrol pipe on a Halley, which we had to braze up.

We arrived at St Quentin, and then went to Bohain and then to Busigny, where we arrived at 3.0 p.m. The people were awfully good to us all the way up and showered flowers and eatables, fruit and drink on us the whole way along, and it was most refreshing as the dust behind one of those columns is awful, especially when one has to pass up to the head, which is very often. Lorries are very hard to pass on a motorbike and one often has to take to the ditch to avoid running into the lorry, as they do not hear one coming up behind. It will be awful on greasy roads, but then there will be no dust. We had a wash and shave in the street of Busigny, much to the interest of the villag-

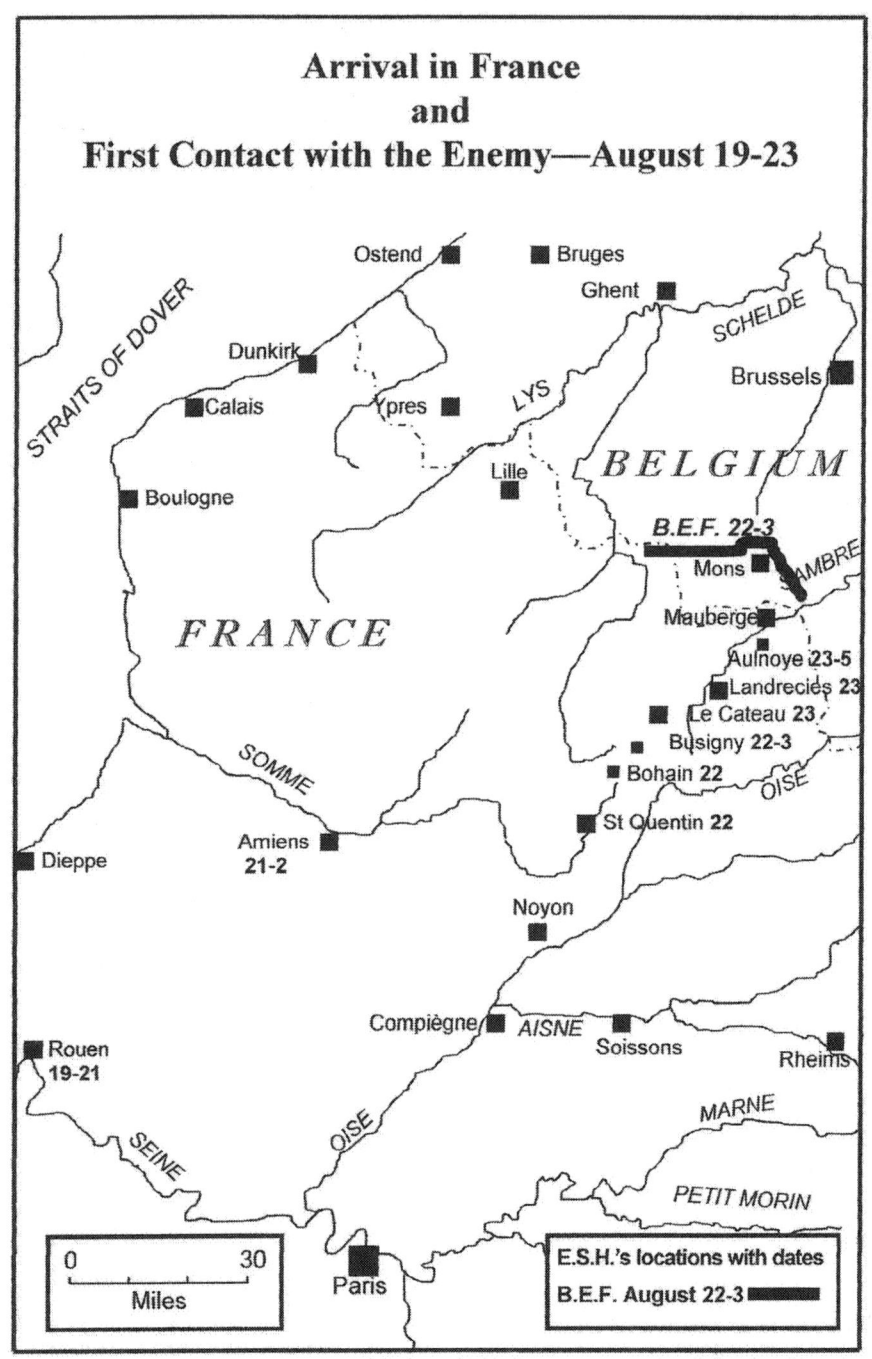

ers, and so we made them boil us some eggs and give us hot water.

> ## Motorbike
>
> The motorbike referred to here was almost certainly a B.S.A. (see p.58). This would have been a 3½ hp single cylinder side valve model with a belt drive and a top speed of 50 mph. A larger version (aimed at the sidecar market) later became the basis of a military model.

We then sat in the car while an admiring crowd of villagers stood round and gazed on us. Among these was rather a pretty girl, and having torn my oilskin I told her to run and fetch a needle and cotton and sew it up, which she did, much to the amusement of the other villagers.

We had some bully and biscuits for supper and then turned in, sleeping in the car. Other columns were continually passing all night, which rather disturbed us. The Halley that was knocking this morning got within twenty yards of Busigny and then put its big end through the crankcase, and so had to be abandoned.

Sunday August 23rd

We set off at 7.30 a.m. via le Cateau and Landrecies to Aulnoye, where we arrived at 10.45 a.m. At le Cateau one of our Leyland lorries stripped its front tyre.

> ## Leyland
>
> The Lancashire Steam Motor Co., set up in 1896 at Leyland in Lancashire produced its rudimentary petrol driven machine (the 'pig') in 1904. In 1912 a bonneted 3 ton truck was approved under the War Office subsidy scheme, and this became the famous RAF type. In its final form this had a 34 hp engine, cone clutch and 4-speed gearbox driving a double reduction bevel rear axle. Over 5,500 of these trucks were built.
>
> Note the reference to the stripped tyre. Most truck tyres would not at that time have been pneumatic, but made of solid rubber.

We left the Q.M.S. [*Quartermaster Sergeant*] and a lorry to pick up rations and petrol at Busigny and to follow on, but its steering gear broke and it leapt

German and French Strategies

The Germans were haunted by the spectre of having to fight a war on two fronts and in the years preceding the Great War made extensive plans to avoid this. With Russia and France allied together, the only way of preventing this was to knock one or other of them out of the war within the first few weeks. The Germans decided to strike at France first, on the grounds that Russia with its inefficient command structure and vast distances would take as much as six weeks to mobilise. This was the famous Schlieffen Plan, which aimed to eliminate France from the conflict with a rapid encircling movement through Belgium and round the back of Paris. The main bulk of the German Army (seven-eighths) was to be committed to this, with only minimal holding forces elsewhere.

The plan was the brainchild of Alfred von Schlieffen, who was German Chief of Staff from 1891 to 1905. It was based on Hannibal's defeat of the Romans at Cannae, but he hadn't enough divisions to do an encircling movement on the left as well as the right, so he put everything into his right wing, which was designed to destroy the British as well as the French, should they enter the war in defence of Belgium neutrality. 'When you march into France let the last man on the right brush the Channel with his sleeve.' The plan was breathtaking in its audacity, allowing just thirty-nine days before the German armies were redeployed to the East to smash the Russian 'steamroller'.

Unfortunately for the plan, Schlieffen's successor as Chief of Staff, Helmuth von Moltke, was a more cautious personality, and couldn't resist sending some divisions to strengthen his left wing, as it were hedging his bets, but in fact weakening the effectiveness of the original plan. He also had to send two corps to the East early in the campaign to strengthen the armies there, as the Russians had mobilised earlier than expected and were threatening East Prussia.

The French also had their plan—Plan XVII. This was based on the Napoleonic doctrine of 'l'attaque à outrance'—attack, all out attack, wherever the enemy is found. So five armies were deployed along the German border and the plan was simply for them to push east to the Rhine. If the Germans really intended to put all their effort into their right wing, then, the French believed, they must be weak in the centre. In fact they greatly underestimated the German strength and their early attacks made only a small amount of headway. Moreover élan (with soldiers in red pantaloons and officers wearing white gloves) was no match for machine guns, shrapnel and an entrenched enemy, and the French casualties in the first few weeks of the war were horrendous.

over a twenty foot precipice. No one was hurt but we could not recover the lorry. After Landrecies a Halley had a blow back in the carburetor and caught fire, but luckily we had fifteen gunners on board, who collected dust from the side of the road and smothered it. But then we had to clean the engine.

Had a row with a postal corporal at le Cateau, who took offence at my oilskin. This afternoon I went off north on my motorbike to look for our Ammunition Column. I went to Maubeuge and had an omelette and coffee, of which I was

---

5th Cavalry Brigade

This is the first mention of any attempted contact with the 5th Cavalry Brigade, whose artillery E.S.H. was supplying with ammunition. The 5th Cavalry Brigade was an independent command and not part of the Cavalry Division. It comprised three cavalry regiments, the 2nd Dragoons (Royal Scots Greys), the 20th Hussars and the 12th (Prince of Wales) Lancers, together with J Battery Royal Horse Artillery, 4th Field Troop and 5th Signal Troop Royal Engineers and 5th Cavalry Field Ambulance. It was commanded by Brigadier-General Sir Philip Chetwode, a dapper Etonian cavalryman, known throughout the army as 'the Bart'. Later in the war he commanded XX Corps in Palestine under Allenby, breaking the Beersheba Line and capturing Jerusalem. From 6th September 1914 5th Cavalry Brigade was linked with 3rd Cavalry Brigade to form the independent Gough's Command, which became the 2nd Cavalry Division on September 13th.

Having completed its landing in France by August 14th, the B.E.F. moved up to the Belgian border and concentrated in the area between Maubeuge and le Cateau. It had General Charles Lanrezac's 5th Army on its right flank. By the evening of August 22nd the B.E.F. was in position around Mons. 5th Cavalry Brigade was on the extreme right of the British line to the north-east of Maubeuge covering the bridges over the Sambre at Binche and Péronnes.

---

in sore need as I had not eaten since 6.0 a.m. and it was now 5.0 p.m. Maubeuge was strongly fortified and full of French troops and all the country round was wire entangled and cleared. I went north but could not find the Column, and when it was dark I started back, took a dry skid on the way, but did not hurt myself as I fell on a French sentry. The French were retiring rapidly. Goldsmith and I had some bully and biscuit, washed our feet, and then went to bed in a very comfortable billet, and I was jolly thankful to get a bed again. Today we heard the guns in the distance for the first time.

Monday August 24th

Had breakfast and went off at 7.0 a.m. on my motorbike again to look for

The Battle of Mons

The gunfire that E.S.H. heard was from the battle which took place throughout August 23rd around Mons. The Germans began their attack on the B.E.F. at 9 a.m., with II Corps bearing the brunt of it. The British rifle fire (15 aimed rounds a minute) caused heavy losses amongst the attackers. Indeed because of it the Germans were convinced that the British had far more machine guns than they actually had. In the end it was the German artillery fire rather than the infantry attacks which caused the British to withdraw from their positions along the canal to a prepared line of defence south of Mons among the pit villages and slag heaps. This began around 3 p.m. and was carried out with great skill under heavy fire. In the early evening the Germans broke off the attack, having sustained over 5,000 casualties. British losses were 1,600 killed, wounded and missing, with practically half of these from just two battalions (400 from the 4th Middlesex and 300 from the 2nd Royal Irish).

the Column. I went first to Pont and then to le Longueville, where I was told I could not go north as the Germans were nearly on us. So I went east towards Maubeuge and by a lucky chance picked them up at Hautmont (just south east of Maubeuge). Having got in communication with them I returned to Aulnoye by 10.0 a.m. I then sat in the garden of one billet and talked to the owner of the house, who was quite a pretty young girl. The railway station was packed with refugees of all kinds, who were in an awful state, and it was pitiful to see them. There were lots of them coming down by road all day, whole families in big carts. The French were retiring through Aulnoye all to-

The Start of the Retreat

E.S.H. here finds himself caught up in the 'Retreat from Mons'. It was about 4.0 a.m on 24th August that the B.E.F. began to withdraw, covered on the left by the cavalry. The withdrawal was brilliantly executed and few Germans realised that the B.E.F. had gone until morning. The officers and men of the B.E.F. could not understand why they were retreating as they thought they had beaten the Germans, but the French 5th Army on their right had started to withdraw thus exposing their flank. This had already begun on August 22nd, with the French being forced back from the Sambre by the weight of the German 2nd Army (see also Diary entry for August 23rd). Throughout the 24th and 25th August the B.E.F retreated south with the men exhausted by lack of sleep and marching. The weather was still hot and the roads thick with dust. The German 1st Army closely followed and attempted to work round the right flank of II Corps and thus envelope the B.E.F. This was prevented by the British cavalry acting as a screen.

day, and we heard heavy gunfire in the distance all day. In the evening we went out in the car to the flying camp and got there just as they were moving off in retirement. A monoplane got up and was not going well, and went through four telegraph wires and four electric light cables, and came down an awful smash and was absolutely smashed up, but no one was killed. On the way back we burst a tyre and had to put on the spare wheel.

Pom kept us amused by reading us extracts from his diary, which was rather amusing. We had a good meal at the railway station tonight. Wrote home. Yesterday the Schweppes Halley broke a front spring, so we patched that up today.

> ### The Schweppes Halley
> This is the first mention of the 'Schweppes Halley'—possibly a requisitioned vehicle from the firm of Schweppes with an enclosed body, as E.S.H. and others used it later as sleeping quarters.

Tuesday August 25th

After breakfast I took our men in arms drill and put them through the handling of a rifle. As our infantry were retiring through Aulnoye and we had no orders, we wired to Headquarters for orders, but could not get through as the wires had been cut by the aeroplane last night.

At 12 noon the whole of our infantry had retired through Aulnoye, so I went out to look for our Column and found them at Blamath (?), and told them that we were retiring to Maroilles via Taisnières where our Column stopped. At 12.30 we started, having a very slow march and getting in at 3.0 p.m.

Here we parked and got a good billet, and were just having tea when there was an alarm and we were told that the Germans were within two miles of us. We waited and were told to fall out and go back to our billets. We had to shift our lorries to another place, and while doing this there was a very heavy storm and we got wet through. Goldsmith and I had just settled down on a couple of sofas at 10.0 p.m., having got into dry clothes, when we were ordered to move off. Goldsmith went off to see the General in charge of the Brigade, which was in Maroilles. I went out and got the engines going, but my motorbike would not start until I changed the plug.

I forgot to mention that heavy gunfire and rifle fire had been going on all the evening, getting closer and closer until it was almost in the village. Goldsmith came back and said that the village was completely surrounded by Germans, who had been brought up quickly in motor lorries, and that they held all the bridges except one. Earlier in the afternoon we had orders to proceed to Etreux, but sent a message back saying that we were wanted by our Column to fill up. It was lucky we did not go back this afternoon as we should have gone through Landrecies, which was in German hands.

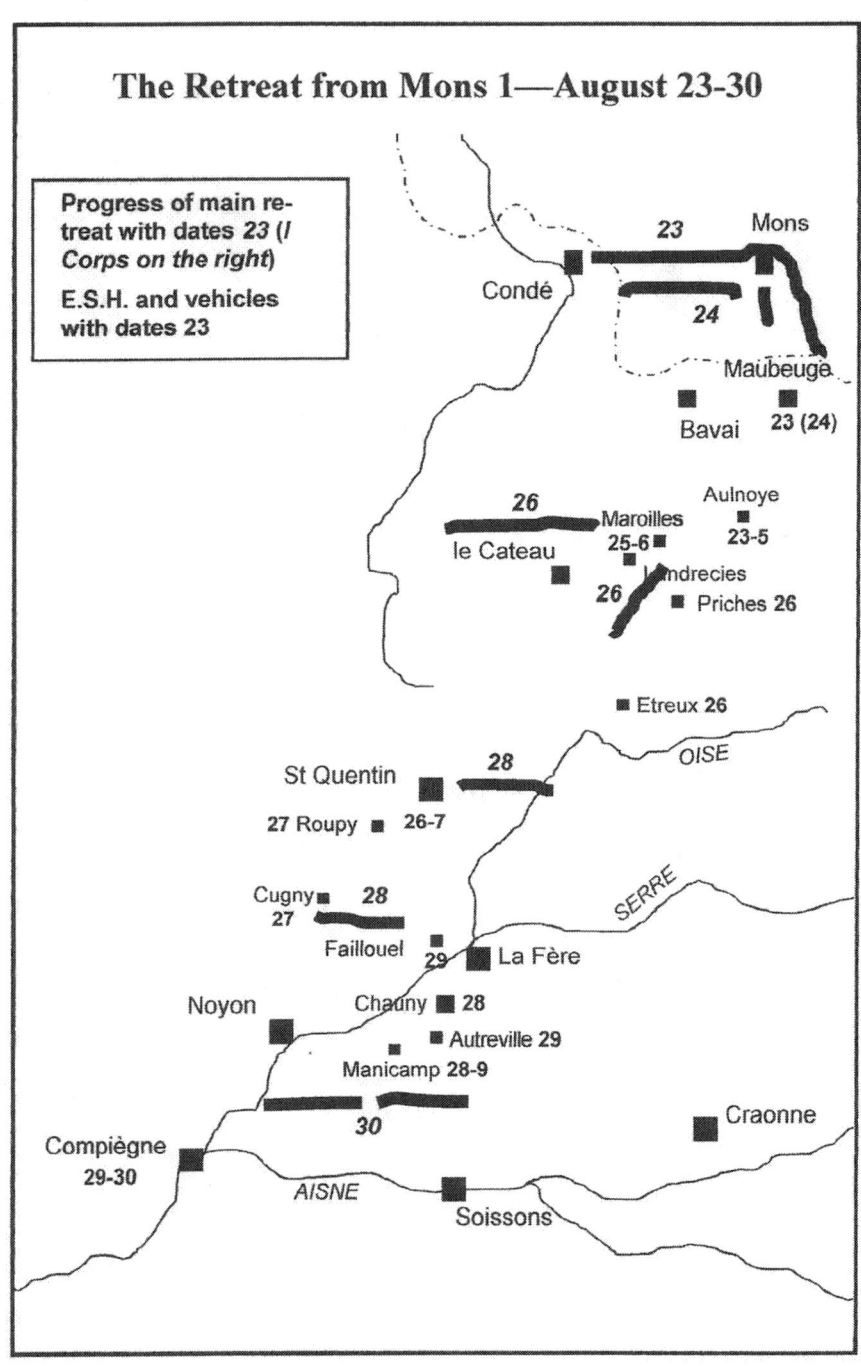

Wednesday August 26th

We had great difficulty in turning our lorries as the road was narrow, and at 12.01 a.m. we started off in the rear of horse transport at one mile an hour and got over the bridge alright. Maroilles was shelled just as we got clear and the Germans were in there an hour later. I was very sorry for the little servant girl we left in our billet, as she was terrified and worked very hard for us. It was a pitch black night and the roads were in an awful state after the rain, added to which we were allowed no lights. Our only orders were to follow the horse transport, and we were the tail of the column and there was heavy rifle fire on each side of the road about a quarter of a mile off. I had to ride my motorbike at the tail of the column and it was not at all a comfortable position, especially when one of our lorries went into the ditch and I had to stay and extricate it. When we had gone about three miles, three of our lorries got ditched and I was an hour getting them out, and did not feel at all safe or secure as we had no escort and only our drivers to help in case of attack.

At dawn I found myself with nine lorries on a road, not knowing in the least where I was going and no one in front of me. I had become separated from Goldsmith and five lorries when the three went into the ditch.

The Battle of le Cateau

Because of the condition of his troops and the closeness of the Germans, Gen. Smith-Dorrien, commanding II Corps, decided to make a stand at le Cateau, in spite of being ordered to continue the retreat. The Germans began a series of attacks from 6.0 a.m. on August 26th and the battle continued throughout the day. Once again the fire discipline of the infantry and the close support of the artillery broke up the German assaults. The artillery in particular played a significant part though heavily outgunned and in exposed positions. Great courage was shown in trying to save the guns, the teams galloping through the cornfields under heavy fire, but 38 pieces were lost. II Corps also suffered 7,812 casualties, but the action enabled them to continue the retreat unmolested. Von Kluck, the German commander, was convinced that he was fighting the whole B.E.F.

I went on for an hour and then ran into Priches, which was full of French troops, and so we were safe. I then made my way back to Etreux, where we were supposed to be, and I had not been there an hour before Goldsmith turned up with the other five lorries. On the way to Etreux I stopped at Boué and picked up petrol and rations. We got a billet and had a wash at 11.0 a.m. They gave us some eggs and jam and tea there, which was most acceptable as we had not eaten since our high tea at five yesterday. Goldsmith and I then slept for a couple of hours in the car, and then I went out north to look for the 5th Cavalry Brigade. Just outside Etreux our guns had taken up a position almost on top of our trenches and on the north side of the town, and later on we lost sixteen of them, as they could not get away through the town. There was nothing between these trenches and our cavalry, a matter of ten miles, and it was not a very nice motorbike ride.

I saw the General, who told us to retire at once to St Quentin. So after a cup of tea and some bread and jam we started off at 4.30 p.m. We had a heavy shower of rain on the way and arrived at 7.0 p.m.

The Action at Etreux

The Editor can find only the briefest record of this action and it does not accord with the description here. E.S.H. was in the line of the retreat of I Corps, which was in better condition than II Corps which had suffered heavily at Mons. At Etreux the 1st (Guards) Brigade fought a sharp rearguard action. Following this I Corps came away safely, apart from the 2nd Munster Fusiliers, who, with 2 guns of 118th Battery R.F.A., were surrounded and fought for 12 hours before the few survivors gave in.

We had been on the go for thirty-six hours, practically without food, and suddenly I began to feel dizzy, so dashed into a pub, which was handy, and had a couple of vermouths, which successfully pulled me together. We went down and had a jolly good dinner at the Terminus Hotel and then came back and slept in the car, and it rained all night. Smith D. was also dining there.

Nice day for Scrummie's birthday, wasn't it?

[*'Scrummie'—Adeline, the middle one of E.S.H.'s three younger sisters*]

Thursday August 27th

We were awakened at 6.0 a.m. by a brass hat, who told us to go west to Roupy, eight kilometres away, and await orders, so I went off on my motor-bike to find the way etc. I met Caulfield in St Quentin and the whole of the 5th Division marching in, which had been going all night and had had very heavy losses. We got to Roupy at 9.0 a.m. and then had breakfast, John Holden joining us as his Column had left him last night. We were having breakfast by the side of the road when there was a very heavy downpour of rain, which drenched everything. I finished my food under a lorry, but my tea which was left outside was drowned. The infantry kept passing at the bottom of the road, and they were dog tired. Last night they had been told to retire and scatter, and half of them had lost their units and did not know where to go.

At 12 noon we moved south west to Cugny, arriving there at 2.0 p.m., and having to go through horse transport, which delayed us a lot. Robinson was there in charge of 3rd D.A.P. [*Divisional Ammunition Park*]. We saw Warren

> ## The 5th Division
> [*See previous page*]
>
> *The 5th Division had been on the right of the line at le Cateau and had been doubly enfiladed. In consequence retirement was extremely difficult and was only achieved by the devotion of two battalions who sacrificed themselves in forward positions. There was considerable confusion as the main road down which the Division retired was severely congested, causing units to be scattered and badly broken up. But there was no irremediable disorder, no panic. On the 27th they halted for a couple of hours in St Quentin, and then with a much needed meal inside them, went on their way, halting at Ollezy on the Somme. Stragglers however continued to come in, and it was at St Quentin that Major Tom Bridges from the cavalry rearguard came across the remnants of two battalions from the 4th Division. The exhausted men were lying down in the town square. They told him that their two commanding officers had promised the town mayor that their troops would surrender rather than have the town destroyed by more fighting. This was not at all to his liking and with the aid of a drum and penny whistle from a local toyshop, he got the men moving again and marching south. The two officers concerned were later cashiered, though one of them, Colonel Elkington, was later given back his commission after joining the French Foreign Legion as a private and conducting himself with great bravery.*

and had a chat with him, and then with the Mayoress, who said that Robinson was dining there, so would we? We went over there at 7.0 p.m., and the Mayor was there, and they did us very well on soup, eggs etc, and a light and good wine to drink. We had some very good liqueurs, brandy with our coffee, which cheered us up a lot. I was the only one who could talk French, so had a very amusing time pulling their legs by misinterpretation. The Mayor and Mayoress were very nice, and she told me of her experiences in the 1870 war, as she had the Germans there and she was very much afraid of them. I was very sorry for her as the Germans were there next day.

Friday August 28th

We were asleep in the car and were awakened at 1.0 a.m. by Robinson's engine starting up. I went over to see him and found that he had orders to go at once to Coucy-le-Château, some twenty miles south. We considered it unsafe to stop there, so followed him out and went to Chauny, ten miles south. It was a miserable trek, as it was pitch dark with a thick mist and we did not know the road. We arrived at Chauny at dawn, and Goldsmith and I went on a petrol hunt and eventually found some together with food at the station. We met Hamersley here with some tractors, and gave him some tyres for his Vulcan. Goldsmith and I then slept for an hour in the car, and then a French officer's wife sent us a message asking us up to her house to wash and have a cup of tea and bread and butter. She was very kind and talked English quite well. We then had our proper breakfast and were told to go to Manicamp and await orders, which we did and arrived at 10.0 a.m., having picked up petrol and rations at Chauny.

Here the French doctor's wife offered us the use of her house, and insisted on feeding us, which was very nice of her. She was married to an English soldier in the South Staffords in the Boer War, where he was killed, and then she married the French doctor, who was a bit of a painter and had some quite good work. She was English but could not talk it. She took us in and gave us some hot water, and we had a grand shave and wash, which was needed as we had not shaved for three days. She had invited two pretty young girls to lunch, who were quite good fun, and I scored over Goldsmith as he could not talk French. We had a very good lunch, after which Goldsmith made himself comfortable on the drawing room sofa and I went into the garden with Madame and the girls, but I am sorry to say they left early and so I went to sleep. I could not sleep as brass hats kept driving up in cars and asking questions. They had a full size bath here and plenty of hot water, so at 6.0 p.m. I had a good bath and change. At 7.0 p.m. I had to go into Compiègne, forty-six kilometres away for orders, so Madame gave me some eggs etc and wine before I left. It was a beastly ride in as it was cobbles nearly all the way, but once when I was on a decent bit of road I was taken unawares by a French sentry, and as I was doing forty, I only avoided being stuck with his bayonet by locking my back wheel. I arrived at G.H.Q. [*General Headquarters*] and waited two hours, when I was told the General could not see me, so I had better go to bed. I said my bed was forty-six kilometres away, and so they said they would wire instructions in the morning.

Nice wasting several hours of sleep and doing ninety-two kilometres for nothing. I left at 11.30 p.m., first having had a whiskey and soda to cheer me on my way. I had a rotten ride back, as I was passing though our lines for the first twenty-six kilometres, and was continually being pulled up by sentries, added to which the road was pavé. I was going north east, and from Noyon to Manicamp I did not meet a soul, but the road was good, so I could get along at a good pace. I got to bed in the car at 2.0 a.m., and just before I went to sleep I heard an airship overhead.

Saturday August 29th

I was woken up at 4.30 a.m. and told to take two lorries of ammunition to the 3rd Cavalry Brigade at Faillouël about ten miles north, as they had lost their Column. We had to go without breakfast and arrived there soon after 6.0 a.m. At 3rd Cavalry H.Q. I was told to go to a village three kilometres north with my lorries, so I followed Bennett with three supply lorries. This village proved to be the most advanced post of our cavalry and had one squadron in it. They had killed fifteen Uhlans here during the night and one of them was fading away on a piece of grass with a bullet in his tummy.

> **Cavalry Encounters**
>
> *August 28th saw an attempt by the German cavalry to exploit the 15 mile gap between the two Corps of the B.E.F. They thrust into the gap in two columns, both of which were foiled by the action of the British cavalry. The 4th Hussars from the 3rd Cavalry Brigade and 'E' Battery R.H.A. quickly ambushed and checked the western column. A few miles away at Cerizy units of the 5th Cavalry Brigade took part in a spirited action against the eastern force. The German advance was checked by dismounted fire from the Scots Greys, supported by 'J' Battery R.H.A. Then Brigadier General Chetwode sent the 20th Hussars to the left and the 12th Lancers to the right to envelop the Germans, who were forced to withdraw. The action culminated in a cavalry charge by a squadron of the 12th Lancers in which seventy or eighty of the enemy were speared. E.S.H. seems to have been involved in the aftermath of the 3rd Cavalry Brigade's action. He does not give the name of the village, but it was at Benay that the 4th Hussars ambushed an advanced party of Uhlans. However that took place at 1 p.m. not during the night, and Benay is not on the canal and some six kilometres north of Faillouël. So it looks as if he is referring to a different incident in a different village—probably Jussy, which is in the right location on the St Quentin Canal. Uhlans were German lancers, but as all German cavalry carried lances, the name was often applied to all of them.*

I had just started moving the ammunition, when our maxim started outside the village, and everyone got on the move. Hearing that we were attacked by a division of Uhlans, backed up by infantry, Bennett and I turned our lorries and went back to 3rd Cavalry H.Q., I going on ahead with a message for the General. Bennett arrived one lorry short, so I went back to the village to look for it, but he had only miscounted. It was while I was coming away from the village for the second time that the bridge over the canal a hundred yards north of the village was blown up, and this delayed the enemy by ten minutes. I went on one or two messages and then found that my lorries had gone south with the Supply Column, so I had to catch and stop them. I then went back for orders and was told to wait at Autreville. Here I met Craven (in charge of the Cavalry Ammunition Column), which was what the 3rd had mislaid. I slept in the ditch for an hour, and then at 1.0 p.m. went into a pub and was going to ask them to cook me an omelet when I saw Craven, and he offered me some lunch. It turned out that two R.H.A. officers of the 5th Cavalry Brigade had had a lunch cooked there, and were just getting down to it when they were ordered to reinforce the 3rd, and had to leave it; for which Craven and I were quite thankful. We had a very good lunch, after which I went up and saw the General of the 3rd and told him where his Column was. I then rejoined my Park, which was refilling its Column one mile south of Autreville. At 4.30 p.m. we started for Compiègne, and after having gone some miles south, we passed through our infantry lines, and then we went pretty well west. We arrived at 8.0 p.m. and then Goldsmith and I went up to the hotel and dined with Mayne, and had a jolly good dinner; after which we went to H.Q. for money etc, and Goldsmith got two 1,000 franc notes for the men's pay etc.

Sunday August 30th

This morning I spent trying to buy maps, as we had come off ours, and then tried to change the notes. The banks had flown, but I managed to change one of them at the post office, and to get some small change from shops and private houses. Met many people here.

Pom and I and the men had a lovely bathe in the river, and at 2.0 p.m. we moved off south to Nanteuil. One of our Halleys broke its timing gear wheel so had to be abandoned. At Crépy, half way, we picked up two lorries from Hewson to replace duds, and here I met Tapy, who gave me some tea. We arrived here rather late and parked and filled up with ammunition. I was ravenous and ate half a tin of bully. Slept in the car.

Monday August 31st

We had to take down a Leyland radiator, so did not get away till 9.0 a.m. I tried to send off a wire but found the wires cut. The whole road was greasy pavé, and the Karrier broke spring brackets and had to lightened. Coeuvres was thirty miles north east and we arrived at 1.0 p.m. Here we found that we were three miles north of our Column, and so it was no place for us, and we went back to Nanteuil.

Hay went into Compiègne today on the Schweppes for the lorry that broke the springs. He found it evacuated. He requisitioned a car at Coeuvres. Troops were retiring hard all day.

Tuesday September 1st

Thinking that we were safe and well in the rear, we took down four engines this morning to clean out, and this of course is a fairly long job. The whole of the inhabitants had the jumps and panicked and told us the Germans were quite close, but we paid no attention to them. Then the railway trains came in and the people said the Germans were quite close, so we just put out a few pickets as a precautionary measure. At 11.0 a.m. a train arrived and said that it had been fired on by Germans a few miles off, so we thought we had better start putting our engines up again so as to be ready to move if necessary. We got the engines up by noon, and, as we had a hot dinner just ready, we had that and then moved off at 1.0 p.m. Here we had a row with Hay, so he left us. We had not gone five kilometres when an aeroplane came down in a cornfield and smashed itself up. The R.F.C. [*Royal Flying Corps*] officer told us that there were three hundred Uhlans and four guns in Nanteuil and no fighting troops between us and them; so we moved off to St Mard near Dammartin. We were rather lucky to have left Nanteuil when we did, as if we had stayed there another fifteen minutes we should have been scuppered. We parked outside the station and then the French built a barricade in front of us and facing us about fifty yards off. We did not like this at all, because if they fired in the night, they would have hit us, so we moved inside the station yard.

Took over two Hallford lorries and changed our Leyland front wheels off one of Scott's duds. This Leyland of ours had done 350 miles without a tyre and mostly on pavé.

> ## Karrier and Hallford Lorries
> *Clayton & Co. of Huddersfield started making Karrier trucks in 1907. Those early Karriers were noted for their hill-climbing and manoeuvrability. Bonneted models appeared in 1911 and by 1913 Karrier were building War Office subsidy trucks. J & E Hall of Dartford started producing Hallford lorries in 1907. In the War they concentrated on 3 ton subsidy models, powered by Dorman engines.*

At 10.0 p.m. we started for Mitry, and one of our Leylands ran into my motor-bike and lifted it ten yards into the ditch, so I had to ride on a lorry. We arrived at Mitry at 1.0 a.m. and had awful trouble getting through the barrier, but eventually they let us through. There were two French regiments and lots of artillery there.

Saw O'Mahoney today. He was captured yesterday with three lorries, but got away again today.

Wednesday September 2nd

It was a boiling hot day. A German aeroplane came over at a great height and all the French wasted their ammunition at it. The French were on tenterhooks all day and every cloud of dust they saw they swore was Germans and kept taking up a defensive position. We moved off at 3.0 p.m. behind Perry's column and they crawled along like snails. We came to one bridge, which the French had mined and were just going to blow up, and we had great difficulty in making them let us pass, as there was a certain amount of danger of a premature. We did not reach Maule until 9.0 p.m., and I had a rotten ride in the dark without a light. Goldsmith and I had some bully and drank Toby's health and then went to bed. [*'Toby'— Leila, E.S.H.'s youngest sister*]

> ## Developments—September 1st
>
> *September 1st was notable for a number of important developments. General Joffre began to reorganise his forces and prepare for the decisive counter-attack by starting to form a new 6th Army under General Maunoury. This would operate on the left flank of the B.E.F. But if the Allied left flank was to be held then it was imperative that the B.E.F. remained in position and did not retreat beyond the line set by their French colleagues. Sir John French, in command of the B.E.F, seems to have lost his nerve at this point and on August 31st sent a long telegram to Lord Kitchener announcing his intention of withdrawing the B.E.F. from the line and retreating behind the Seine. Kitchener immediately came to France and persuaded French to fall in with Joffre's plan.*
>
> *Meanwhile the B.E.F. was showing plenty of fight. A surprise attack by German cavalry at Néry on units of 1st Cavalry Brigade and 'L' Battery R.H.A., who were watering their horses at the time, was turned from disaster into a notable victory. What should have resulted in the severe defeat of a British brigade ended with the smashing of a German division, with three V.C's amongst the officers and men of 'L' Battery.*
>
> *It was at this point too that the Germans began to make a series of errors. The German 1st Army began a turning movement away from Paris and in front of the B.E.F and the French 5th Army, because its Commander, General Alexander von Kluck, believed that the B.E.F was beaten and thought that he could now decisively strike the French in the flank. He was also worried about the gap that had developed between his army and that of General Karl von Bulow . It was this movement which began to expose the whole of the German right flank to the Allies. It also signalled the virtual abandonment of the Schlieffen Plan,*

Thursday September 3rd

We did not move, so I spent the morning looking over my motorbike. Saw lots of people as it was a big railhead. Yesterday Bell and L.G.Humphries were taken prisoner with five lorries. We had a hot bath in the Schweppes and both caught cold after it.

Our tractor drivers were nearly captured at Manicamp, but mounted some German horses which had stampeded and got away. They rejoined us today.

Friday September 4th

Moved off at 6.0 a.m. and arrived at Mormont at 7.30 a.m., and had a very nice place to park. Went into G.H.Q. at Melun on my motorbike and bought some vulcanising solution. Had a good lunch and bought some cigarettes.

Had a swollen gland and an awful cold.

Goldsmith and I went up to 5th Cavalry Brigade at Coulommiers and lost our way. We saw them shelling Coulommiers, which they had been shelling all day and only hit one horse.

Maule

[See entry for September 2nd]

E.S.H. gives no explanation for this surprising move to the west of Paris, well away from the B.E.F.'s main line of retreat. Possibly the situation was so fluid and uncertain to the east, that this was considered the safest and most sensible route.

Saturday September 5th

Left at 7.0 a.m. and arrived at Melun at 8.0 a.m. and parked near the railway station. Had a shave in the house opposite and then slept and had lunch. Hay is still missing—peaceful. Hard pressed this morning at 6.0 a.m. and again in a wood at 7.30, but quiet since. Town fairly large but empty. Bought some sardines, biscuits etc.

Hay rolled up this evening. Slept in car. Rifle inspection.

Sunday September 6th

Got up at 5.0 a.m. and had breakfast at 6.0 a.m. A very hot day. Saw Tapy, Saulez, McCaskill and others. Saw Savage off to Le Mans, the advanced M.T. base. No move.

The End of the Retreat

On September 5th the B.E.F. finally halted on a line some fifteen miles south east of Paris. They had retreated nearly two hundred miles in thirteen days, with an average of three to four hours sleep a day. Casualties were 15,000 killed, wounded or missing and the artillery had lost 42 guns. But the men recovered quickly and reinforcements had already arrived at the end of August, making it possible to form III Corps.

Monday September 7th

Had to buy rations for the Company. Meat very dear - veal 10, mutton ¼, bread $2^2/_3$. Had a bathe. Cold much better. Had bacon and tomatoes for

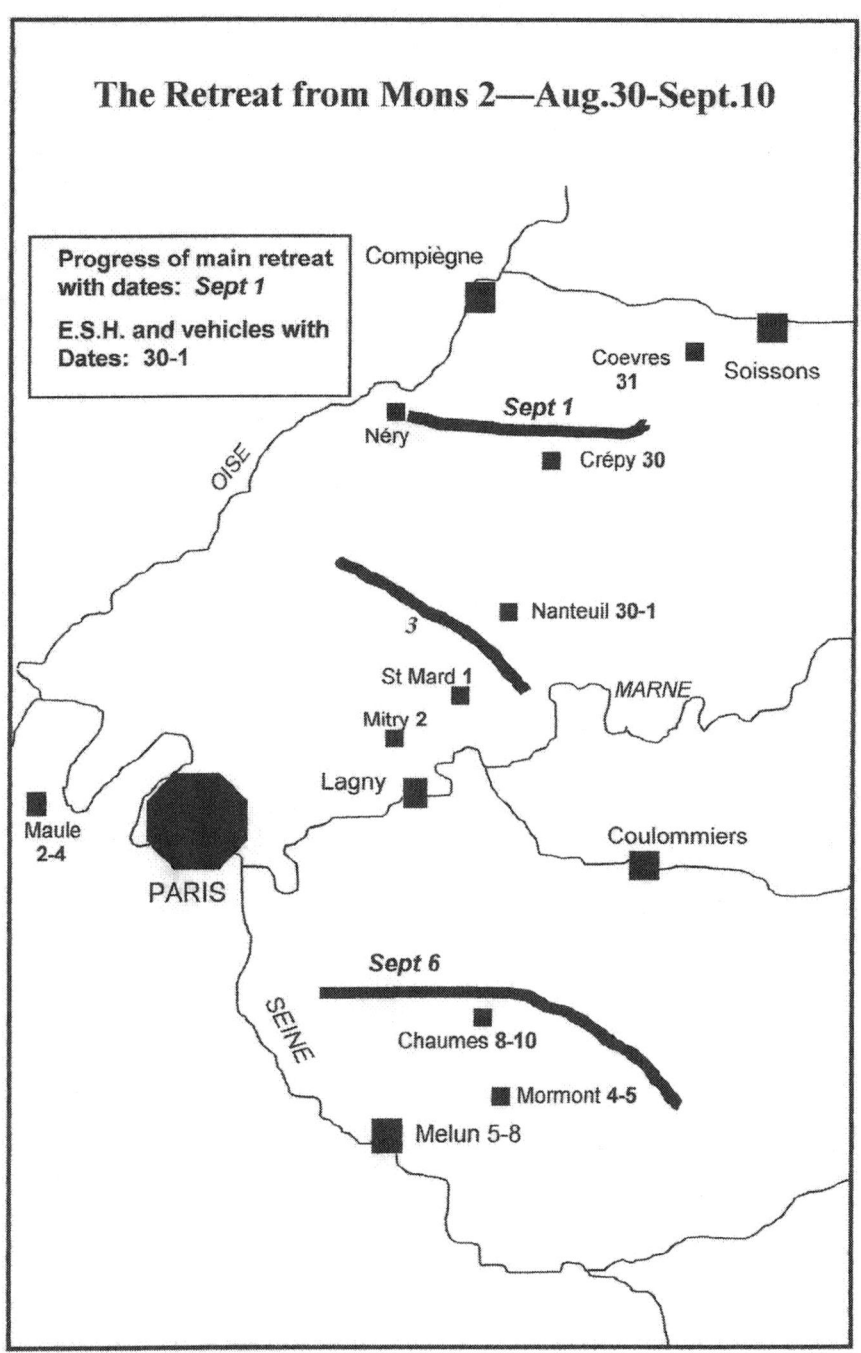

breakfast. No letters received yet. One lot of mail bags were burnt to avoid capture by the Germans. Fearfully hot.

Walked through the town in the evening and had a drink with the owner of the house opposite our Park, and talked much to them. Had an amusing chat when buying chocolate for the Company.

Hay cleared off on a job at about 2.0 p.m. T.G. was hosed while shaving.

Melun

[*Ville Romain*—*from a postcard found tucked into the pages of the War Diary*]

Melun was an important railway junction south east of Paris, and the site of the British G.H.Q. at the end of the retreat, and further back than Field Marshal French had originally promised. On September 5th, Joffre motored the 100 miles from his own H.Q. to Melun to make a personal appeal to French to play a full part in the planned offensive. His appeal succeeded and the B.E.F. started moving forward on the following day.

Tuesday September 8th

Had breakfast at 6.0 a.m. and left Melun at 6.30 for Chaumes, where we arrived at about 8.0 a.m. Met Allden en route. Monsieur and Madame saw us off from their window in nighties.

Went up to a farm to buy food and got twenty-three rabbits, and my arm ached with killing them. The owner had two big farms and all hands have deserted, taking horses etc with them, so he is in a bad way and will lose a lot as he can't look after his stuff. Cold beastly.

We started to advance today, thank goodness. Weather still glorious, only a nice breeze today. All clothes being aired in the sun. Drove into Melun with Saulez to buy tyres and dined. To bed at 10.30 p.m. Cold cured.

The Battle of the Marne—September 5th-9th

This was less a battle than a series of manoeuvres and engagements, which resulted in the Germans losing the strategic initiative. For the B.E.F. the advance was a matter of route marches, bridging rivers and streams, with a number of firefights with the German rearguards. On 9th September the B.E.F. crossed the Marne and continued the advance. Unfortunately the Allies were unable to exploit their victory by a rapid advance. The troops were tired and the field commanders cautious. So the Germans retired in good order to the river Aisne, which they made their main defensive position. The Allies reached the Aisne on September 11th and 12th.

Wednesday September 9th

Went to Headquarters at Coulommiers and waited for five hours. Awful smell en route from dead horses and cattle. Returned at 4.0 p.m. Villagers are returning and farm labourers are back.

Thursday September 10th

Cold alright. Left Chaumes at 7.0 p.m. and came to Coulommiers. Smell still bad near the woods. Went into H.Q. and had a quiet day. At 6.0 p.m. we received sudden orders to supply ammunition at Dammard fifty-eight kilometres from here. Started at once and had a miserable journey over frightful roads in the dark. The roads were very narrow and greasy with very soft ground on the sides. We followed 5th Supply Column and many of their lorries got ditched. I drove the car, while the rest slept, including Pommier who came in our car.

Friday September 11th

Arrived at Passy-en-Valois at 3.30 a.m. and issued ammunition. Started for home at 5.15 and arrived at 10.0 a.m. Had a wash and breakfast and then lay down at 11.0 a.m. 12.30 p.m. had lunch and then rested till 4.0 p.m. Then tea.

It rained most of the way back and then there was extraordinary heavy rain all day. Had the Schweppes (covered lorry) fitted up for our use and it was quite comfy as we could get both valises out flat with room to spare. After tea I walked down to see Perry and then came back to supper and bed. Heavy rain during the night. Three lorries arrived (Hallfords) with 13 pounder ammunition for 3rd Cavalry Brigade, which I took over. Got into pyjamas for the first time since August 24th.

---

13 Pounder Ammunition

This would be for the Royal Horse Artillery, which used 13 pounder quick firing guns. The Royal Field Artillery used 18 pounder field guns (see page 27), though some territorial units attached to infantry units had 13 pounders. The shell fired by the 13 pounder gun was 3 inch calibre (76mm) and weighed 12.5lb (5.7kg). It had a maximum range of 5,900 yards (5.4km), with this distance being covered in a little over 10 seconds. These two guns were adopted as standard by the Royal Artillery in 1904 as a result of the Army's experience of modern enemy artillery in the Boer War.

Saturday September 12th

Woke after a good night's rest, had breakfast, washed and shaved. Wasps awful. Saw Allden. Lorry no. 58 had broken its reduction gear wheel on the way to Dammard on the 10th, so found a dud Leyland and removed its wheel and sent it out to ours at C (?) [*Illegible*].

Weather might clear, it is trying hard. Cleared up and went down to H.Q. Had lunch and started at 1.15 p.m. for Nogent with four lorries to fill with ammunition. I went in the car thankfully.

Arrived at Nogent at 3.30 and found no ammunition. Took over two lorries full of 13 pounder ammunition from Spafford and filled one of mine from his third as it was a dud. Had a drink with Spafford and tea and proceeded home at 5.0 p.m., arriving at 7.15. Leyland 58 came with me. It rained all the way home. Had supper and a cigar and it rained like hell. A mail bag had arrived—our first lot—and I received six, dated 10th to 22nd August.

Sunday September 13th

Heavy rain but the Schweppes does not leak. Paraded at 7.15 a.m. and went to Nogent. Togged up in overalls and so of course the rain stopped. The roads were very bad for a motorbike and I slipped much, especially on cobbles. Saw Clarke at Coulommiers and gave him a cigarette.

Left two lorries at Nogent to fill with ammunition. Proceeded to Latilly and arrived at 12.30, passing many dead horses, which were so, so. Goldsmith and I visited the village and bought an iron for five centimes and vegetables.

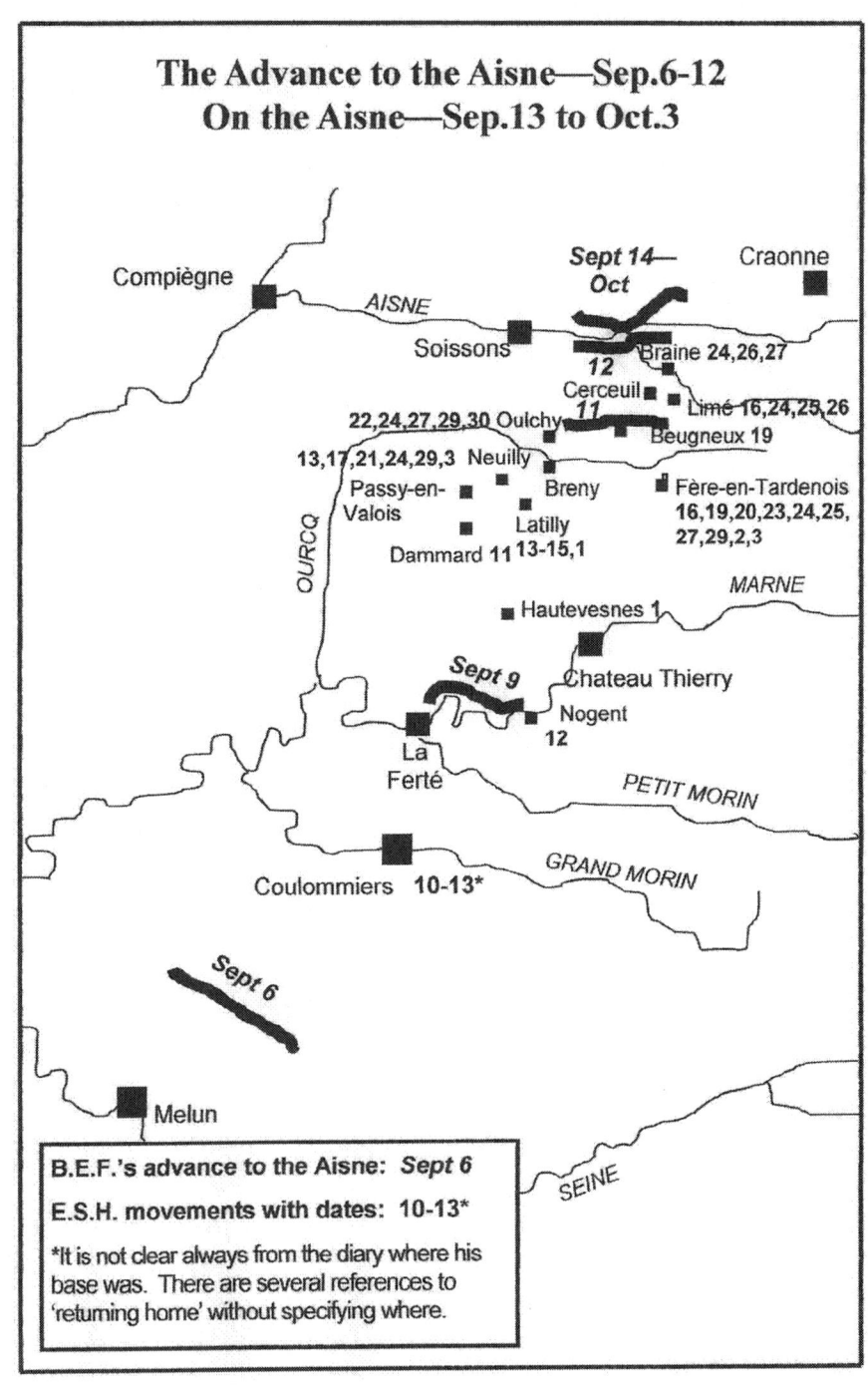

> ### Artillery on the Aisne
> [*See next page*]
>
> *The B.E.F. experienced less difficulty than expected in crossing the Aisne on September 13th. Although the bridges had been destroyed, the troops managed to get across in rafts or by makeshift repairs to the bridges. However once across they were subjected to punishing artillery fire. The 3rd Division (mentioned here), which established a bridgehead at Vailly, was checked by fire from the German heavy guns. Because of the slowness of the pursuit the Germans had been given time to dig in on the heights on the far side of the Aisne. A 17th century carriage road runs along this escarpment known as the 'Chemin des Dames', and it proved to be an impregnable position. At the same time the Germans had brought up their heavy 8 inch howitzers, which had been used in the reduction of the fortress of Mauberge, and the allies found themselves at the receiving end of artillery much heavier than their own. This is significant in that it marks a change in the balance of power on the battlefield. In the past victory had usually depended on a mastery of the 'all arms' battle, finding the right combination of infantry, cavalry and artillery, but now artillery was beginning to dominate the battlefield. More than 60% of casualties in World War 1 were from artillery fire. The infantry's answer was to dig trenches, and the battle on the Aisne marks the end of the war of movement and the start of trench warfare.*

The people got very excited in their speech and said the Germans did not pay for food but these officers did.

Had dinner at 4.30 p.m. and tea immediately afterwards, and then I took the car and went over to see Perry at Neuilly three and a half kilometres off and arrived back at 7.0 p.m. Bought half a dozen eggs and had them for supper. Very fine evening. Washed feet.

Monday September 14th

Very heavy rain all night and early this morning; still looks doubtful. Sent twenty men to a farm nearby with Hay, which was reported to be occupied by Germans. They drew blank. Hay and Goldsmith have gone off to see General Gough.

We parked outside the village last night and our lorry pulled up just alongside the grave of a German soldier. When I put my head outside this morning before breakfast, I saw one of the villagers at work digging him up, as he said he was not deep enough. Turnbull had a very bad pain and almost collapsed, so we sent him off to hospital in a lorry. Goldsmith and Hay were away all day so Pommier and I had a long talk. He is a very good fellow and quite sensible and not over excitable. The rain stopped at about 11.0 a.m., but it has been

> ### 'Gough's Command' and the 2nd Cavalry Division
> [*See previous page*]
>
> Brigadier-General Hubert Gough commanded 3rd Cavalry Brigade in August 1914. On September 6th this was joined with 5th Cavalry Brigade to form an independent formation known as 'Gough's Command'. This in its turn was constituted as a Division on 13th September and Gough was made a major-general. On 14th October the Division was further strengthened by the transfer of the 4th Cavalry Brigade from the original (now 1st) Cavalry Division. These units were then formed into the Cavalry Corps under Lieutenant-General Edmund Allenby. 56 MT Company A.S.C (E.S.H.'s unit) formed the Divisional Ammunition Park for the 2nd Cavalry Division.

windy and stormy all day. French bread is very nice but will not go far enough. The ration of bread is 1 lb per day, and I can eat 1 lb a meal if it is new, which it always is. It is not nearly so heavy as English bread. Goldsmith arrived back at about 7.0 p.m.

German big guns 90lb very much in evidence and have bust bridges. 3rd Division over river, rest not. Daimler broke spring shackle; forged new one.

Tuesday September 15th

Waited till 11.0 a.m. for one or two repairs to be completed. Moved to Breny at 11.0 a.m. over a very bad road indeed (almost impossible on a motorbike). Had dinner at 1.0 and then went in the car to Nogent to fill up two lorries with 13 pounder ammunition, which had been sent on previously. Met the whole of 6th Division marching up, and overtook one lorry with broken steering in between Château-Thierry and Nogent. Left the men on the lorry (a Halley) to guard it.

> ### 6th Division
>
> This peacetime division was quartered in Ireland and England at the outbreak of war, and was ordered to concentrate near Cambridge. By early September it was fully equipped and trained. On 10th September 1914 it landed at St Nazaire and proceeded to the Western Front. The division arrived in time to reinforce the hard-pressed B.E.F. on the Aisne. Earlier on 30th August Lieutenant-General Pulteney had arrived to form III Corps, which consisted initially of the 4th Division and the 19th Infantry Brigade, pending the arrival of the 6th Division.

Filled up at Nogent and came home, arriving at 7.0 p.m. It rained all the way home. Heavy guns going all day.

Wednesday September 16th

Moved off at 7.30 a.m. with five lorries to Limé near Cerseuil to fill up with ammunition and arrived at 10.0 a.m. Filled up and then went to Fère-en-Tardenois to H.Q. and refilled two lorries from the railway.

Met Saulez and had a glass of beer (muck). Arrived at Breny at 3.0 p.m. and had lunch. Sergeant Major took twenty-five prisoners this morning. At Fère-en-Tardenois I saw a horse that had been skinned and disembowelled—I wonder why they did not do it before.

Went to Neuilly this evening to see Perry and saw Dunphy. Received the *Times Weekly* for 4th September today. Drank Dad and Mum's health.

Thursday September 17th

Got up at 5.30 a.m. and paid out after breakfast. Shaved and read the *Times*. Very wet. 6th Division passed through yesterday. Sent down and put in a new steering gear for a Halley off a dud and got a new spring. Rained hard all day but cleared up in the evening.

Paulimier had tea and a long talk with us. Smoked my last cigarette. Went to Neuilly-St-Front this evening and saw Perry.

Friday September 18th

Went into H.Q. at 7.30 a.m. Blocked on the road by a Bulgar, who had long hair and was very grey. Saw Matthews. Disembowelled horse still there and getting rather fruity. Rained all the afternoon but cleared a bit in the evening.

Fetched the mail from H.Q., but there was none for me. Rained all night and the guns fired all the time. I saw the flashes twenty miles away. Took photos.

Saturday September 19th

It stopped raining about 6.0 a.m. Got the mail off the train—received one postcard from home. Went into H.Q. and picked up a taxi which did a two mile trial well. Left Randall to bring it home and came back. As Randall left Fère-en-Tardenois the back axle broke. Picked up a back axle from a dud at Beugneux, five miles from here (Breny). Passed the skinless horse again today. Piff! Piff!

Sunday September 20th

Went up to H.Q. at 7.45 a.m. in the car with artificers in a lorry to mend the taxi. Rained heavily all morning. We experienced much difficulty in fitting the axle as the wheels are of a different pattern, but eventually managed it by building up the back axle, half from each car and of different lengths.

Came back at noon; the taxi and lorry arrived at 4.30 p.m. Discovered that the taxi has no cushion yet and two windows broken. Must see to this. Received a letter from Uncle Arthur [*see below*]. Goldsmith got some Gold flakes—good. Got ½lb of shag each for cigarettes issue. Drew two days groceries from Fère-en-Tardenois. London Scottish arrived—very military? Had a buck with a major about potatoes and kilts. The shag cigarettes are not bad, better than the French though strong. Saw Gilpin this morning at 8.30 a.m.

London Scottish

The 1st battalion of the London Scottish was a territorial unit, which moved to France and became G.H.Q. Troops on 16th September. Kitchener was not in favour of the territorials, and they were sometimes referred to disparagingly as 'Saturday night soldiers' by regulars. This may account for the slightly mocking tone here. However they soon proved their worth in battle and came to be highly regarded. This particular battalion was the only reserve available when the Germans attacked at Messines on 31st October, and was brought forward to assist the 2nd Cavalry Division, to which it was then attached. In the ensuing battle it acquitted itself well, with something like 30% casualties. General Allenby noted in his report: 'Rarely, if ever, have second line troops sustained unshaken so high a percentage of casualties'.

Monday September 21st

Rained last night but was fine though cold this morning. Went down to the station for mails but there was none there. Goldsmith has gone to Neuilly-St-Front for mails. The artificers are at work tuning up the taxi.

The taxi was running this afternoon but had a jump into first gear owing to a gummy clutch and no clutch stop. Thinned the oil in the gearbox and it went much better, but it is very cramped from the driver's seat. Bought some spuds off the mayor and some planks of wood. The mail arrived tonight and I got a postcard and letter from Mum, dated 29th August. Wrote a semi-French letter to Scrummie and Fuzzy, and to Uncle Arthur and Mum, and also to the O.C. [*Officer Commanding*] A.S.C. Bulford about kit. [*Uncle Arthur—Arthur Hacker RA (1858—1919) was a well-known artist, known for his figurative works, portraits and landscapes. Many of his paintings are still in the family. For Scrummie see page 36. The Editor has no idea who Fuzzy was.*]

Crowds of wounded have been coming in ever since we have been here, and we have heard the guns going in the distance all day and night. I hear tonight that the Germans are retiring again, but whether there is any truth in it remains to be seen.

Received a free issue of the *Mirror* for 10th September and the *Chronicle* in which there was General French's first dispatch.

> ### Fighting on the Aisne
>
> *The initial fighting on the Aisne, when the allied forces were attempting to drive the Germans from the heights, was very costly. On September 14th, for example the 1st Cameron Highlanders lost 600 men, almost 80% of the battalion, and six other battalions in Haig's Corps lost more than 300 men apiece. Casualties were fewer in the 4th and 5th Divisions, but the 3rd Division lost over 1,000 men. The 'Official History' describes the situation on the Aisne front after September 15th as 'The Deadlock', and that was how it remained—with both sides entrenched with little change geographically until 1918.*

Tuesday September 22nd

A very fine morning and it has the makings of a glorious day. It is very silent and I have heard no guns since last night.

Went over to Oulchy-le-Château and bought cigarette papers, dishcloths, envelopes and an eggcup. Tidied up and swept the Schweppes and put in a couple of shelves. Went for a walk after tea and had a buck with Major Cowan at the railway station.

In the shop at which I bought the eggcup there was a very pretty girl, but I did not have time to talk to her as Goldsmith was with me, but I will buy a teaspoon tomorrow perhaps. Lots of wounded are still passing through.

Wednesday September 23rd

Sent off a lorry to fill up with ammunition at 7.0 a.m., and then strolled over to the station where we got a *Daily Mail* for the 22nd. At 10.0 a.m. Hay returned from H.Q. and handed over the park to Goldsmith as he has been ordered down to the Base.

At 10.15 a.m. I went up on my motorbike to issue ammunition, but could not find the lorry, and after looking about until 12 noon I came back. I was just about to send out another lorry, when the other one returned empty, and I suppose I had missed it. After lunch Paulimier and I went into H.Q. at Fère-en-Tardenois for letters, but there were none. We were greatly hampered both going and coming back by French troops, crowds of which were moving from the right of the line to the left, where I hear 250,000 have lately concentrated owing to some movement or other. Of course now Hay has left us Paulimier (Pom) will live with Goldsmith and me. Tonight at 8.0 p.m. Jesse came to us and said his car had broken down and that he wanted to go into H.Q. So I drove him in and got back at about 9.0 p.m. Bought two dozen eggs.

> ## Outflanking Movements
>
> *With the Aisne line stabilised, a series of outflanking movements began between the French and German armies. If one side could get ahead of the other there would be a chance that they could roll up the opposing line from the flank. So the 'Race for the Sea' ensued, with each side attempting to outflank the other, but always being stopped by an opposing manoeuvre. At this stage the B.E.F. remained dug in on the Aisne, but it was not long before Field Marshal French began to consider the possibility of moving the B.E.F. to the left of the French armies, so as to be closer to the Channel ports and his supply lines. General Joffre did not like this, but the B.E.F. was an independent command, and on October 1st the Field Marshal told Joffre that he intended to remove his force from the Aisne to a new position north of La Bassée, and Joffre did not oppose this.*

Thursday September 24th

Yesterday morning like this morning was very cold, almost freezing, but it was a glorious sunny day with no wind, and I think the weather has changed for the best. This morning Goldsmith, Pom and I went into H.Q., but there were no mails. We saw Matthews and Goldsmith got 2,000 francs from the cashier. We then went on to Limé and issued 600 rounds of revolver ammunition. From here we saw about half a mile away some of our shells bursting near a German aeroplane, but it got away. Yesterday we saw one of our monoplanes chasing and rapidly overtaking a German biplane, but we thought they were both English or we should have followed in the car.

From Limé we went on to Braine to 2nd Cavalry Division H.Q., and there I saw Warren and had a long talk with him. On the way home we called in to see if there were any letters for us at La Siège, 5th Cavalry Brigade H.Q., but there were none.

After lunch Pom and I went off to Neuilly-St-Front, where I bought some sardines and strawberry jam, and then we went on to Oulchy-le-Château, where I bought two eggcups and had my hair cut in a little barber's shop (not so bad). The taxi went quite well and will I think be alright. Goldsmith paid out tonight. Smith washed quite a lot of my clothes yesterday.

Friday September 25th

Had breakfast at 6.15 a.m. and Pom was half an hour late. Had a shave and complete wash and then went to H.Q. with Pom in the taxi and picked up some oil and flannelet, which we took up to the Column at Limé. Staff Sergeant Bentley came in too with reduction gear for the Wolseley to tune it, but could not get hold of a small enough emery wheel. Saw twelve or eighteen

> **Wolsely 3 Ton Lorry**
>
> *The Subsidy Class A Wolsely was one of the first types built to meet War Office requirements and was first produced in 1913. It marked the firm's return to lorry building for a short period and many hundreds were used on the Western Front.*

shells bursting at a German aeroplane. Saw Gilpin and Matthews. Got the mails, very small—one from Kath and also a charm—touch wood—thanks [*Kath—Kathleen, the eldest of E.S.H.'s three younger sisters*].

Returned in time for lunch. After lunch took two lorries and 103 cases of 13 pounder ammunition to 1st Cavalry Division A.P. [*Ammunition Park*].

Much hampered en route by 6 D.A.P. Saw A.G. and went to Laird at H.Q. to pick up a new gunner, a second lieutenant, and he seems alright. Had tea with Laird and again on arrival here. Pom accompanied me.

Goldsmith had a bath today so there are not so many flies in the Schweppes. When I have my bath there will be fewer still.

Saturday September 26th

Had breakfast at 6.30 a.m. and then Goldsmith and I went into Fère-en-Tardenois in the taxi and filled a lorry with 40 boxes of revolver ammunition, which we took up to the Column at Limé.

We saw shells bursting in the same place as yesterday, and that is three days we have seen them. We came to the conclusion that they are German shells fired from a long distance and bursting too early and high and practically harmless. We saw them even from Breny, where we are parked early this morning.

I picked up the mails and received a nice long letter from Mum dated September 12th. We came back through Braine but saw nothing of interest and called in to see Morrison and Spafford on our way back as I wanted a motor horn off him.

We came back by Fère-en-Tardenois and had lunch with Laird while the lorry was getting 100 gallons of petrol and 8,000 rounds of revolver ammunition. We got back at 3.0 p.m., and then found a shed in the village and I got an old woman to heat some water for me and I had a grand bath. The place was rather dirty and there were some rabbits in a hutch in the corner, but it was very refreshing. I had not had a bath since September 3rd, after which I caught a bad cold, but I had this one earlier in the day while the sun was up.

Had a *Daily Telegraph* today for September 17th. A German aeroplane came over us early this morning. There has been very heavy gunfire all today and yesterday and all night. The French are still moving over to the left and one army corps passed through today.

Saw McCaskill today and his car has been replaced by a Baby Peugeot. He went up to his unit and was fired at point blank from a wood by two Germans south of the river. John Reckitt made a smart capture of four Germans the other day. I saw five guns of 113th Battery at Fère-en-Tardenois, which had been very badly knocked.

> ### 113th Battery
>
> *The Editor can find no record of any engagement in which 113th Battery lost five of its guns. 113th Battery was part of XXV Brigade Royal Field Artillery and was attached to the 1st Division, which was on the right of the line in the advance to the Aisne, so would have passed close to Fère-en-Tardenois. However there is no record of any engagement there. In fact September 11th, when the B.E.F. advanced beyond Fère, was particularly quiet, the main problem being congestion on the roads. Shortly afterwards 113th Battery took part in the attack across the Aisne on September 14th, but again there is no record of damage to their guns. R.F.A. batteries had an establishment of six guns, and to have five put out of action would surely have been reported. Perhaps after all they were not so badly damaged as they seemed to E.S.H..*

Sunday September 27th

Breakfasted at 6.30 a.m., but Gottswaltz had a cold and did not appear till 9.30 a.m. Today was not a very nice day and rather overcast. The meat was very late coming today, so we had boiled bacon and vegetables for lunch, so I did not eat very much as it was rather fat. After lunch I had to go up to our Cavalry H.Q., so I took the Vauxhall and Pom came too. First we called at Oulchy-le-Château and then Breny and left a pair of my boots and one of Goldsmith's to be resoled. We then went on, calling at farms to buy eggs, but could get none. I delivered my dispatch at Braine and then went on to G.H.Q. at Fère-en-Tardenois, and on the way met Jenkins and Lonpeigne. On our way back we managed to get 23 eggs. I met Parkin at Braine.

Spy scare - stopped by a sentry in broad daylight.

Monday September 28th

There were a few letters for us this morning and Goldsmith got two, but I drew blank. He also got twenty cigarettes and gave me ten, so we enjoyed a decent smoke again. It was ripping smoking an English cigarette again. I spent the whole morning writing my diary and letters.

Gottswaltz went up to Braine today. Major Cowan got hold of a gun and seven cartridges today and he and Goldsmith went out to shoot hares, but got none. It was overcast all day and looks like rain. Very heavy firing this evening. The flies are simply awful and we kill hundreds every morning and evening when they are stupid with cold.

After lunch another mail came in and I received three letters and Goldsmith none. Mine were two from Dad, dated September 3rd and 21st and one from Mum dated September 18th.

Goldsmith cut his own hair a few days ago with a pair of nail scissors, and finished it off with a razor. Now when he gets up first in the early morning and looks fed up and combs his hair straight, he looks just like Peter Dooley, the jockey, in *Merry and Bright* in the *Arcadians*. I wrote a long letter to Dad this evening. [*The Editor would dearly love to know more about Peter Dooley etc, but research into music hall turns of the period has produced no further information.*]

Two German spies have been flying about our lines in a red cross lorry, one dressed as a woman, the other as a civilian, but they have been caught and shot. There are still two more at large in a car. So we can't get into Fère-en-Tardenois after 6.0 p.m. and have to carry passports.

Spies

There seems to have been something of a spy scare around this time, caused in part by German officers who, with great courage, had elected to stay behind disguised as civilians. There were also others who were in the pay of the Germans. Elaborate telephone installations, leading from haystacks and cellars, showed the ingenuity and foresight of the enemy. However, in the prevailing atmosphere of suspicion, a number of innocent people were certainly also executed—mainly by the French, who appear to have been none too particular as to their methods in their anxiety to stamp out the danger that spying posed.

Tuesday September 29th

Some English papers for September 23rd and 24th arrived today and we shared them. Read and wrote my diary all morning. Gottswaltz and Pom went up to Cavalry H.Q. in the taxi with pistol ammunition, and the taxi crown wheel bolts sheared.

After lunch I went into G.H.Q. with letters and received a letter from Tapy's sister. Bought some sugar and gave it to Mathereuse at Oulchy-le-Château. Received pipe baccy and a cardigan from Dad and chocolates, Keetings, canned soup, postcards and hankeys from Mum. Walked to Oulchy in the evening with Goldsmith and bought some eggs.

Wednesday September 30th

No mails for us. I wrote my diary and inspected the taxi. Pom and I went to Neuilly-St-Front and picked up a taxi wheel. We bought eggs. Posted letters at G.H.Q. and bought some jam. Came home via Oulchy-le-Château. Must see the abbey there.

Thursday October 1st

Went to Latilly for four tyres for the taxi and got a spare wheel for the B.S.A. I gave the interpreter a clasp knife. Went to Grisolles for the wheel. Looked for Tapy but could not find him. Beautiful day—very cold with early frost but very warm at midday. Went to Cavalry H.Q. at Hautevesnes. The cavalry are all round here and just west of Oulchy-le-Château. Reserve parks are retiring to make room for 2nd Corps, which is in reserve. There was a block on the road.

Phillimore and Clarke had tea with us. Saw Tapy at Grand-Rozoy. It is cold tonight.

Friday October 2nd

[*Only scrappy notes for this day*] Rifle inspection. Clean up. Horses. Cold now, no sun, mist. Letter from Uncle Arthur. To Fère, Gilpin, car. Phil. Move. Pheasants. German aero.

Saturday October 3rd

Goldsmith has gone to Cavalry H.Q. Pop and I went to G.H.Q. at Fère-en-Tardenois at 11.0 a.m. We moved at 2.p.m. to Neuilly-St-Front and parked one mile outside the town. Pom and I went out in the car and burst a tyre at Latilly and had to wait for a spare wheel.

The B.E.F. moves to Flanders

On the night of October 1/2 the B.E.F. began to move north. The units left their line on the Aisne in great secrecy, with the enemy unaware that they had gone. First to move was the 2nd Cavalry Division, which went by road. Then II Corps, which left by rail from Compiègne on October 5th, arriving on 8th and 9th. III Corps followed, then I Corps. G.H.Q. moved to Abbeville on October 8th and to St Omer on the 11th. As can be seen from the Diary, E.S.H.'s Ammunition Park, followed in the wake of 2nd Cavalry Division, arriving near St Omer on October 13th.

Sunday October 4th

Moved to Crépy and waited there for two hours. Got a new Sunbeam there and then moved on to St Just, where we arrived at 4.30 p.m. Dined in the town, which is rather large and slept in the Schweppes. There was a pontoon at Port Salut where we were rebuffed. [*The Sunbeam was a car (see page 78.). Sunbeam, originally a bicycle manufacturer, never made lorries.*]

Monday October 5th

Stopped at St Just. Received a copy of the *Times* and a postcard.

Tuesday October 6th

Set off at 7.05 a.m. for the twenty-five miles to Ailly-sur-Noye. Saw a French field butchery unit. Arrived at 10.a.m. It rained. We had a tea party.

Wednesday October 7th

Got up at 5.0 a.m. Moved off at 8.0 a.m. and arrived at Amiens at 10.05 a.m. One of our lorries' back axle went and it ran back down the hill. We towed it in. Inspected Bertie's 50 and made good use of spare wheels and other parts.

Had a hair cut and shave and bought necessaries. Changed car driver. Lunched and dined at Gaby's.

Thursday October 8th

Had a bath in a hotel and a change of kit and felt cleaner. Saw one cavalry officer and the padré in the hospital. Saw Courtenay and spent the afternoon with him. He, Pom and I dined in a café. I took Courtenay home ten kilometres in the car at 10.0 p.m. Pom was jumpy. Lunched at Gaby's.

Friday October 9th

Lunched at Gaby's and moved off at 3.0 p.m. to Frévent. Fair Americans took our photos.

Ten miles out Lorry LN 309 went over a bank down a 10 foot drop and smashed. Taylor was knocked out so I took him in the car and met a field ambulance just outside Doullens. We arrived at Doullens at 7.0 p.m. and dined at the Hôtel d'Amiens. An aeroplane stalked us during the journey.

Saturday October 10th

Goldsmith and I went to G.H.Q. at Abbeville. Gilpin was in a bad temper and liverish—he could not have had breakfast. Got a lorry and I cashed a cheque for £5. Sent the lorry back and took the driver in the car, via Talinas, where I dropped him to sit in the lorry. Had lunch at 2.0 p.m. and met Olga. Saw Spafford. Received 200 cigarettes and the *Weekly Times*. Dined at the hotel and saw Perry afterwards. Had a letter from Kath and a postcard from Mum.

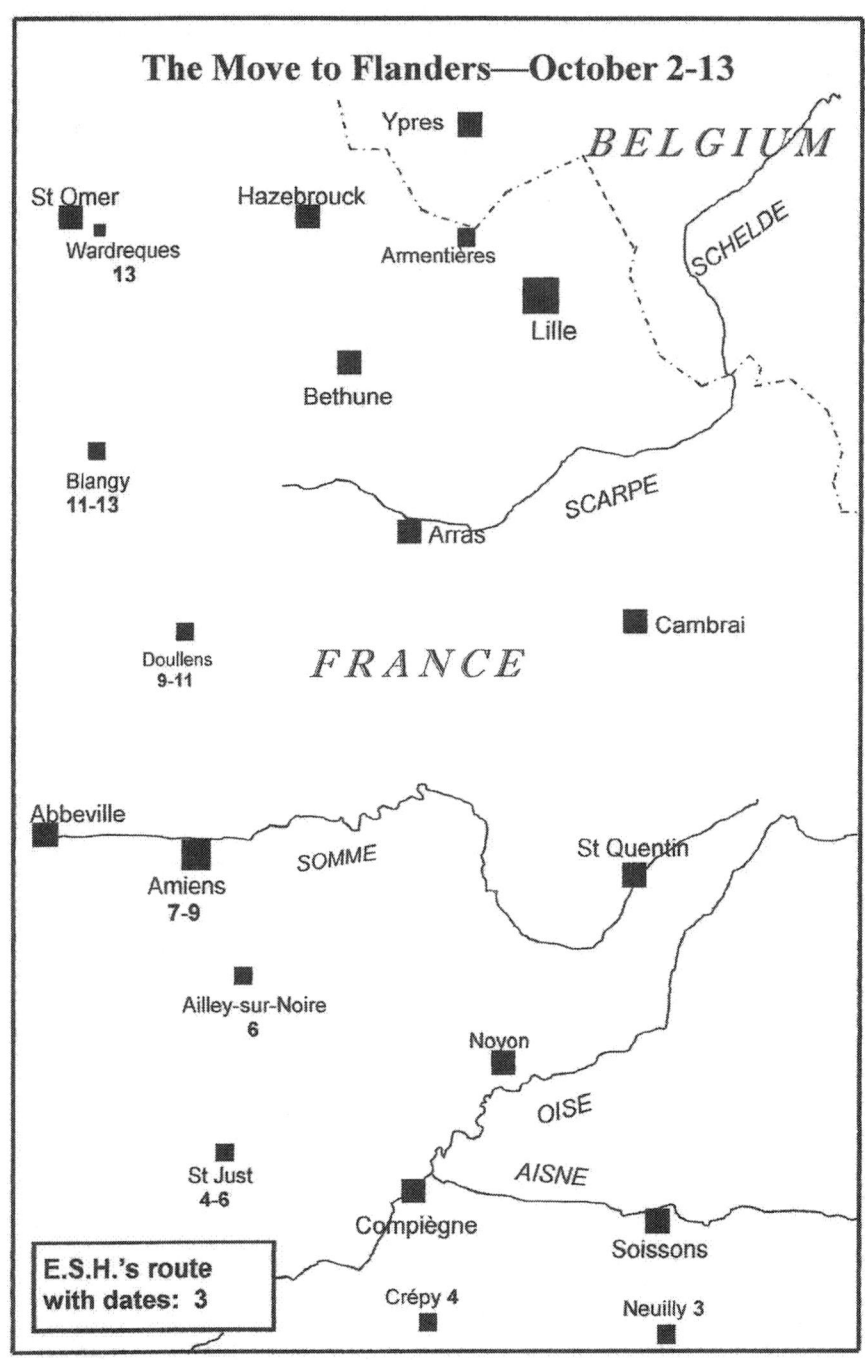

Sunday October 11th

Left at 7.0 a.m. and arrived at Blangy at 10.0 a.m. where we parked.

Received 100 *Abdullas* from Aunt Adeline and a letter from Mum. [*Adeline Hacker, E.S.H.'s aunt, fell in love with a Frenchman, Louis de St Quentin, but he was married already and faithful to his wife. Many years later, when his wife died, they were married, but sadly Adeline died after only a short time with him. A beautiful portrait of her hangs in the Editor's bedroom.*]

On the way we passed a French flying corps and field butchery unit. I took the sitting room opposite the Park and it was very comfy with a fire. Blangy is full of refugees from Lille and Antwerp.

Fall of Antwerp

Antwerp fell on October 10th in the face of overwhelming German forces and heavy artillery. Britain had offered to send the 7th Division, the 3rd Cavalry Division and a number of heavy guns under Lieutenant-General Sir Henry Rawlinson to the relief of Antwerp, but in the event the offer was too late. So the forces landed at Zebrugge and Ostend on October 7th and 8th and moved to join the B.E.F. in Flanders, where they were reconstituted as IV Corps.

Monday October 12th

Remained at Blangy. Sergeant Kestin had a motorbike accident and tore off an ear. It is frosty and misty and cold. Had breakfast in the sitting room. Pom, Gottwaltz and I went to G.H.Q. at Abbeville. for passports etc. There were crowds of refugees on the road and we picked up a French soldier at Hesdin. The French cars are very bad.

We returned by 1.0 p.m. and had chicken for lunch, which was very good. It was lovely and warm in the sun. I ragged Pom and slept on the grass.

Tuesday October 13th

Moved off at 8.0 a.m. and arrived at Wardrecques at 12 noon. Took two lor-

---

Battle of La Bassée
[*See next page*]

This had begun on October 11th when units of II Corps collided with the enemy. On October 13th the fighting hotted up and Field Marshal French ordered the newly arrived III Corps to assist II Corps. This fits in with E.S.H.'s account as 4th Division was part of III Corps and 5th Division part of II Corps. II Corps continued its offensive over the next few days, and by October 18th had got within a few miles of the suburbs of Lille. But that represented the high water mark of the British advance.

ries to Caëstre to fill up the Column via Hazebrouck. 4th and 5th Divisions are in action close by and heavy guns.

Met Tit Willow and Brooke-Murray. Started back at 6.0 p.m., having had much trouble finding the Column. It was very dark and raining hard there and all day with a bad mist. Horrid road and a Daimler got badly ditched by the front wheels. Arrived back at 8.0 p.m. and had two boiled eggs, having had no food since breakfast at 7.0 a.m. Was rather tired. Received copies of the *Weekly Times* and *Punch* and a letter from Uncle Arthur and Holt.

Daimler

Although the name 'Daimler' is more usually associated with prestigious cars, the firm pioneered the truck industry with its 1896 1½ tonner, and today Daimler-Chrysler (formerly Daimler-Benz) is the world's leading truck manufacturer. Clearly some of its vehicles found their way to France at the beginning of World War 1, though there are no details here. Shortly before this, however, Winston Churchill had asked the London General Omnibus Company to provide some buses (with volunteer drivers and conductors) to provide transport for the Royal Marines' Antwerp operation. The 75 vehicles selected were from the Daimler fleet (see further page 64).

Wednesday October 14th

Left at 8.0 a.m. for Caëstre and arrived at 10.0 a.m. We had trouble with a Thorney and Leyland 57. Heavy rain. The railhead was again changed so we returned to Wardrecques arriving at 1.30 p.m. Had a shave and lunch and then went to G.H.Q. at St Omer for letters. A 'hairy' kicked at our car and covered us with mud but was clear of us. [*'Hairy' is not to be found in the various dictionaries of World War I slang that the Editor has consulted, but*

Cavalry in Belgium

On October 11th Allenby's Cavalry Corps crossed the Belgium frontier and secured Messines and Wytschaete, two villages on the higher ground overlooking Ypres from the south. Next day, with the rest of the Cavalry Corps pushing north, the 3rd Cavalry Brigade made a dismounted attack on the Mont des Cats, a small hill crowned by a monastery, which it captured without much difficulty. On the 13th the Cavalry Corps continued to move north to Berthen, and then turned eastwards towards the Lys. On the night of the 16th an attempt was made on Warneton, where the Germans had a bridge over the river, but they resisted all efforts to dislodge them. From then until the end of the month the cavalry occupied defensive trenches, with the 2nd Cavalry Division to the north of the 1st, between Messines and Hollebeke.

from the context would seem to mean a 'near miss'. This is supported by general slang usage meaning 'dangerous', 'risky'. Compare: 'To make one's hair stand on end.']

Thursday October 15th

Had a misunderstanding with the pig in the farmyard last night, as he chased me when I shone my torch in his eye.

Gottwaltz and Pom have gone up with ammunition. Our cavalry are in Belgium again now and we are driving the Germans back. Gill's interpreter and chauffeur were shot last night by one bullet which went through two doors and three legs.

A new second lieutenant called Anderson joined today. He has a temporary commission for the war and had a job in the Argentine. Morrison came in to tea and Gill lunched here.

Friday October 16th

Still at Wardrecques. Had rifle inspection and showed Anderson round.

Pop and I went to G.H.Q. and had tea there with Pom. Ditmas came out with us and I drove him back in the evening.

Saturday October 17th

Took arms drill at 9.30 a.m. and then Pop, Anderson and I went up with ammunition. Waited for two and a half hours for Pilham, who had been looking for the Column, and then went to Wytschaete (*Flemish Wijtschate*) and filled up. The roads are very bad indeed in Belgium with frightful hills. We started back after dark and went and filled up at Aire-sur-la-Lys and did not get back till 11.0 p.m. Lost a Daimler and a Halley broke a radius bar and two rear springs. Missed a beautiful roast duck dinner. Saw a horse treadmill thresher.

Sunday October 18th

Goldsmith went off at 8.0 a.m. with five lorries to the Column at Wytschaete, and I took the rest of the lorries to Strazeele, our new railhead. It was quite a decent day and Anderson and I had some bully in the Schweppes. At 3.0 p.m. Gottwaltz and I took the empty lorries to Aire to fill up and got back at 7.0 p.m. We have a farm for a billet a quarter of a mile away, and they do us very well. We had hot Mackonachies for dinner. Morrison handed over five lorries today. [*Tinned rations: 'Bully'—corned beef, mainly from Argentine. When company cooks got it, it was served as stew. Otherwise it was eaten cold or fried. 'Maconochies' (note correct spelling)—sliced vegetables, chiefly turnip and carrot in a thin soup or gravy. Named after the inventor or manufacturer. A 'dinner in a tin'.]*

Monday October 19th

Had breakfast in the Schweppes and then took Gottwaltz and Kesting to G.H.Q. at St Omer. The car went excellently. After lunch Goldsmith and Pom went up to the Column and returned at 3.0 p.m., when Pop and I took up ammunition. We met about a hundred London buses full of troops and had to pass a whole divisional train coming back.

London Buses

The usefulness of buses in the Antwerp operation led the army to requisition buses for their own use with the volunteer crews enlisting in the Army Service Corps. To begin with they still had their red and white colouring along with advertisements, but later they were painted khaki. Many were also modified, as ordinary lorries, or as specialist vehicles—ambulances, staff caravans, and mobile pigeon lofts! Carrier pigeons were still a major means of communication.

We came back in the dark and my generator fell off. It rained hard today and the farmer in our billet gave us a very good dinner of roast chicken etc. Received a parcel today containing cocoa, soap, matches, vests and potted meat.

Tuesday October 20th

Got an awful cold. Anderson and Pop have gone off to fetch ammunition at Hazebrouck. Pom has gone to G.H.Q. at St Omer with Kestin. Our guns have been firing hard for some days and we are trying to deceive the Germans and make them think that we have a large force here, when we have only cavalry, as the infantry are not up yet. There was a rumour that five hundred Uhlans had broken through last night, but it did not worry us although there are no troops between us and our line; and of course they had not broken through! Went up to Wytschaete to see if any ammunition was wanted and Anderson and Pot took up five lorries at 3.0 p.m. Harry Wilder visited us at 4.0 p.m. and was quite affable. Goldsmith went to G.H.Q. with Perry. I sat by the fire and mothered my cold by going to bed early. Slept well.

German attack on the Cavalry—October 20th

The Cavalry Corps, numbering around 9,000 rifles, was opposed by six German cavalry divisions and four jäger battalions, a total of 24,000 men. The Germans attacked on the 20th, and the cavalry were driven back, digging in that night between Ploegsteert and Messines. III Corps came to their assistance, and they managed to hold Messines during further attacks that night, but the château at Hollebeke, to the north east, was captured.

Wednesday October 21st

Went to Hazebrouck with Pot and loaded the lorries, but the ammunition train ran out and could not complete us. After lunch we went up to Wytschaete and filled up and returned for a late dinner.

I received a postcard and letter from Kath and copies of the *Weekly Times* and the *Western Morning News*.

Thursday October 22nd

Everyone bar Pom and I went out after ammunition. French and Indian troops were detraining all night.

The Indian Division

This would have been the 3rd (Lahore) Division, which had landed at Marseilles around September 26th. 15th Sikhs were part of the Jullundur Brigade, the first Indian Army unit to land in France. That very night (Oct. 22nd) it moved to the front and acted as a screen for II Corps to withdraw from its exposed situation to the carefully prepared defensive position, later known as the 'Smith-Dorrien Line'. Together with the 7th (Meerut) Division, which had landed at Marseilles on October 12th, it formed the Indian Corps, a very welcome addition to the hard pressed troops around Ypres. Indian Army units were to be involved at the end of the month with the 2nd Cavalry Division in the defence of Messines in what turned out to be a critical few days for the B.E.F.

We were ordered to move to Ebblinghem, our new railhead, to give room for detraining at Strazeele. We met the Indian Division on the road and it looked very fit. Saw Growse in the 15th Sikhs and talked with him for 400 yards.

There was a big block all along the road so we did not get to Ebblinghem till 3.0 p.m. At 4.0 p.m. Anderson returned and I had to go up to help Goldsmith at La Clytte (*Flemish De Klijte*). It was an awful journey up as the lamps kept going out and very often at high speed.

We eventually caught up with the Column at 6.0 p.m. in Belgium and found them blocked on the narrow sloppy road by two hundred French lorries, which wanted to get by, and it took until 10.0 p.m. to get them passed as many stuck.

We arrived at the Column at 10.30 p.m. and had to sleep there. I rigged up chairs for a bed and slept in a horse rug in a farmer's billet.

Friday October 23rd

Off-loaded the ammunition and then went round and saw the batteries in action and filled up the advanced Column. Wytschaete was being shelled, but they were all falling short in a potato patch.

Came back after lunch to our billet in a farm. Had tea with Savage and I talked about the second Mons and partridge shooting with his interpreter.

Received a parcel from Mum—socks, films, matches, soap, chocolate and a warm waistcoat. My cold has almost gone. Ragged Goldsmith and was hit over the head with a wine bottle. Received a letter from Dad. He is selling the motorbike. Saw Napean, Fitz and Leland. On October 21st the cavalry did a marvellous bluff and kept off hundreds of Germans.

3rd Brigade charged trenches. Second Mons on 21st. Hector's teeth. Guns at 1200 yards.

Battle of Ypres

The Editor can find little that tallies with the rather cryptic references at the end of the entry for October 23rd. However the few days from October 20th witnessed some very heavy fighting, The so called First Battle of Ypres was in fact a series of engagements, some heavier and more critical than others, as the Germans probed the British lines for weak points. It was not until mid-November that things calmed down and both sides accepted a virtual stalemate. Attempts were made to break this stalemate several times later on in the war, but the Ypres salient remained inviolate to the end. Ypres had a significance beyond its strategic importance as the only substantial Belgium town not in German hands.

Saturday October 24th

I thought I liked farm life, but not when the ducks wake one at 5.0 a.m. and quack. Went to St Omer G.H.Q. for headlights. Spent a quiet day. Went to see Morrison at Hazebrouck and had tea there and called at Perry's.

Sunday October 25th

At 9.0 a.m. I went up to Cavalry H.Q. and then went through Wytschaete to the H.Q. of 5th Brigade to see the Field Paymaster and to get some money from him.

A battery was in action there, but things were quite quiet, although we heard a Maxim and rifle fire close by. We went to see if the Column wanted any ammunition and then came back in time for lunch.

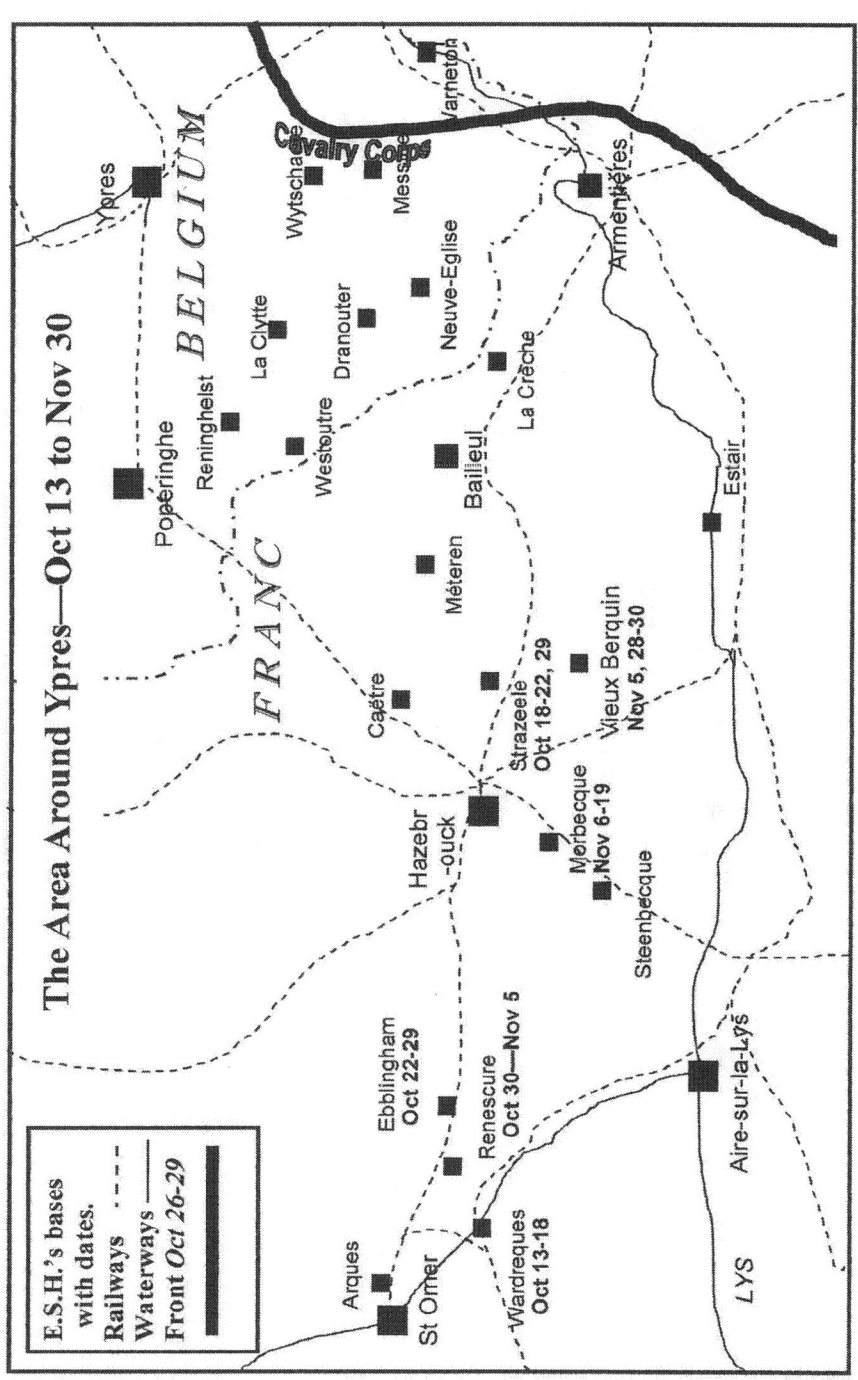

Monday October 26th

Halley rear wheels taken off to be re-tyred and sent down to Paris. Gibbon arrived to take over the Park. After lunch I went to the railhead with Pom and back via Perry at Lynde.

Received two letters from Mum today, dated 1st and 21st October. Issued out 90 cigarettes per man and baccy—a gift. A cow was taken ill with milk fever in the night but recovered.

Tuesday October 27th

Gibbon and Anderson went up with ammunition at 6.30 a.m. 1st Supply Column had a bomb dropped on it yesterday, which did no damage beyond breaking three windows of Major Evan's car, it having burst only twenty-five yards off. [*This presumably refers to the Supply Column for the 1st Cavalry Division.*] Tried to borrow some Hallford back wheels today. Received some cigars and baccy from Dad and clothing for the men from Mum. Went into G.H.Q. to post letters and took Keston into hospital. Indian sentries hunt at night and won't stop still. Can't shake off cold, which still hangs on slightly.

Wednesday October 28th

Went into St Omer with Kestin and met Tapy there. Chased him. Walked up the hill in the afternoon and saw them shelling a German aeroplane at St Omer. Had a grand roast beef dinner and went to see Perry in the evening about moving. I hear that after a night attack a few nights ago 2,000 Germans were buried in one field, and of the 1,000 who broke through our line near Ypres (*Flemish Iepei*), 400 were taken prisoner, the rest being wiped out. Rifle inspection. [*The Editor can find no record of these events*]

Thursday October 29th

Moved off at 8.30 a.m. for Strazeele, where we arrived at 10 a.m., and got a good billet by the railway station. A lorry ran into no.59 and bent its front axle and a Hallford broke its front spring.

Gibbon and I went and looked at a fine château near Strazeele, but we did not billet then, as we heard we are shifting again tomorrow. After lunch Gottwaltz, Pom and I went to Estaires and saw Tapy, who gave us some tea. We had a chat but it came on to rain and was misty coming back.

The lorries all along the road at Vieux Berquin and Estaires are in an awful state and have all been set on fire, and the church is all knocked about. Two bombs dropped on Hazebrouck today. Had a very fine duck for dinner. A German aeroplane was brought down at Hazebrouck today.

Friday October 30th

Moved off at 8.0 a.m. for Ebblinghem, and just as we were nearing Hazebrouck we spotted a German aeroplane coming straight for us. We did not worry about him as there have been several attempts to wreck Hazebrouck railway station with bombs and they have gone nowhere near yet, so he was pretty certain not to hit our Column. Suddenly he turned and fled, and we saw two Britishers after him. We parked at Renescure, three kilometres west of Ebblinghem and have a good billet there in the brewery.

It rained hard this afternoon and was very cold. At 6.30 p.m. I had to suddenly go off with eight lorries of ammunition. The Column is still at La Clytte, which is forty kilometres from here. We had a miserable journey up in the dark and shortly after starting met some Foden lorries, which put one of mine in the ditch.

Foden Lorries

These would have been steam lorries, probably 5 tonners. The Army already possessed a few of these in 1914, but took over very many from civilian firms in late 1914. Foden built its first steam lorry in 1901, and continued producing steam vehicles right into the 1930's

---

We got on alright to Bailleul, where we found two hundred French lorries parked for the night, the road blocked and all their drivers asleep.

I sent for their officer and cursed him in French to the best of my ability and as I had had to go without dinner he was impressed and soon had the road clear. From here on (Belgium) the road is awful and there were blocks the whole way up, isolated lorries being ditched owing to the greasy state of the roads, and two were right across the road.

I arrived at the Column at 9.30 p.m. and had not off-loaded till 12.0. Rifle fire was quite close.

Saturday October 31st

We left La Clytte at midnight and did not get in until 3.30 a.m. We passed a large force of cavalry marching up. The Schweppes had to go up last night, but was not unloaded after all. I did not get up till 7.30 a.m. After breakfast I went to the station and found three Douglases for us and rode one back. [*These were probably 2¾ twin engine machines. They proved very popular and Douglas supplied 25,000 during the War for use by dispatch riders.*]

Anderson went up with seven lorries at 3.0 p.m. this afternoon. Our cavalry are using all this ammunition owing to the fact that they are in the trenches.

> ### Consumption of Ammunition
>
> *Pre-war estimates of the amount of ammunition required by the artillery and infantry were based on the experience of the South African War. These proved to be totally inadequate. In the early weeks of 1914 the British artillery fired more shells than it had done during the entire South African War. In the First Battle of Ypres the British artillery was very short of shells, with some batteries having to ration each gun to a few shells a day. And in I Corps Sir Douglas Haig had at one point to withdraw a third of his guns and send them to the rear as he had no ammunition for them. This was not just a British problem. All the armies of the Great War entered the conflict with far too little artillery ammunition.*

A most extraordinary bird, called Bray, joined us today. He came out as a fitter and got a commission and is an awful fellow. Received two sleeping caps from Dad; very nice and warm for night wear. I was very tired and went to bed early.

Sunday November 1st

At 7.30 a.m. I went up to Arques and loaded up three lorries and had hardly returned when I had to take up six lorries to the Column. The cavalry had been pushed back during the night, and I was not sure whether the road was

> ### The Fighting October 29th to November 1st
>
> *These were days of real crisis, when the Germans mounted a series of heavy attacks on the B.E.F. positions around Ypres. To the north, Haig's I Corps were driven out of Gheluvelt on the 31st and the way seemed open to Ypres itself, but the situation was saved by a weakened battalion of the Worcesters, who counter-attacked and recaptured the village. The main thrust however was to the south-east of Ypres, where a freshly formed German army of seven divisions attacked four very depleted British divisions—the 7th Division and the three divisions of the Cavalry Corps—a numerical superiority of three to one. They held the line against repeated attacks, but were eventually forced to withdraw on November 1st to prepared positions, leaving the villages of Wytschaete and Messines in enemy hands. Meanwhile an appeal had been made to the French for support, and reinforcements of their troops started to come up and take over parts of the line.*

safe or not. I asked a staff officer I met, and he told me that I had better not go my usual way, but as the only other way was very hilly indeed I went my usual way and found it alright. I found that the Column had retired to Reninghelst (*Flemish Reningelst*) and arrived there at 1.30 p.m. I off-loaded and did not get back till about 6.0 p.m., and as I had not eaten since breakfast, I ate a pretty good tea and did justice to some steak at 8.0 p.m. Last night we had a grand dinner of roast pheasants, which Gibbon had shot, and they were glorious.

Apparently the German main attack is against our cavalry and 'black marias' have been falling like hail since yesterday.

However we have not given yet, only bent, and today large reinforcements came up and the French are going to make a big counter attack. Came back via Westoutre (*Flemish Westouter*).

Black Marias

This was one of the tommies' nicknames for the heavy German shells (5.9" and above), so called because they burst with a cloud of black sooty smoke. They are thought to have been named after the police prison van, though the Germans used 'Schwarze Marie' for a heavy naval gun. Other names were 'Jack Johnson' after the American heavyweight boxer, and ' coal-box'. The French poilus called them 'marmites' (cauldrons).

Monday November 2nd

Went into St Omer with Pom and Bray and took Sergeant Kestin to the hospital. Bought some notepaper and then found a parcel awaiting me with a nice writing block. Called at Arques and received 200 cigarettes from Uncle Arthur. Received some pants, mufflers, socks, mitts etc from Mum. Paid out and issued *Daily Sketch* cigarettes to the men. Called in at Wardreques this morning to buy some eggs and they were very pleased to see us and gave us a drop of beer.

Lots of hostile aeroplanes being shelled yesterday. Received a tummy belt from Frizzie and wrote thanking her. Received some films. Lorries did not return till 12 midnight. Beautiful fine moonlight night.

Tuesday November 3rd

Got up before the sparrows at 5.0 a.m. Went off at 6.0 a.m. with three lorries of Q.F. [*Quick Firing ammunition*] to a place north of Méteren. Arrived at 7.45 a.m. Took Parsons round the batteries to see what they wanted. Got one lorry very badly ditched and very nearly dropped it in a river ten feet down, but got it out eventually having put all the villagers on to off-load it. Left two lorries up there and returned by 1.0 p.m. After lunch went into St Omer, had a haircut and shave and then had tea with Ditmas and Switch. 2nd Cavalry have been relieved from the trenches and are now in reserve.

Received a letter from Dad and *Weekly Times* for October 30th. Saw a French aeroplane brought up in pieces in a lorry and in fifteen minutes it had been assembled and flew away. For the last fortnight our cavalry have held a front of ten miles with only 1,500 rifles in the trenches, which is an extraordinary feat as they have been attacked in pretty good force. Pom bought a V.P.Kodak.

Cavalry Numbers

The Editor has some doubts as to the accuracy of this statement in the Diary, as the entire British front around Ypres according to one authority (Robin Neillands) was only 12 miles on October 31st. However the cavalry line was certainly very extended (at least 6 miles according to some maps of the battle). Again 1,500 rifles seems a very small number for three divisions. Robin Neillands also quotes the number on October 20th as being 9,000 rifles (and that was before the 3rd Cavalry Division joined the Cavalry Corps). But there is no doubt that all units were becoming increasingly depleted during this time. A contemporary authority (Sir Archibald Home) gives the numbers for the 1st Cavalry Division as only 900 towards the end of October, and then estimates the casualties during fighting around Messines as 50% —50 officers and 450 men. So perhaps the numbers given are not quite so unlikely as they seem at first sight.

Wednesday November 4th

Had a look round the engines. Went to the station and got a pair of rear Halley springs. Went over to see Morrison re Hallford wheels. and he has four for us tomorrow part worn. Had lunch with Morrison and Spafford. Pom came too. Got two part worn back Hallford wheels from the station. Had a bath, the first since Amiens on the 8th, nearly a month. Find Mother's white socks not half so economical as black ones. Received some socks, mitts and hankies from Aunt Adeline. Beastly dull day and rained tonight.

Thursday November 5th

Took the Park to Strazeele our new rail head, and Pom and I went on ahead to find a billet in Vieux Berquin. The first house we called at there was a woman dying, but we eventually got a decent billet. Was rushing about all the afternoon trying to fit wheels, and had no lunch but an enormous tea. Our billet was just near the church, which had been biffed by three or four shells, but not damaged to any great extent. Had a letter from Mum today. After tea Gibbon and I went off to look at a château at Morbecque, as we are moving there tomorrow and thought it would make a good billet. It was awfully foggy and misty coming back and one could hardly see the side of the road. Ate half a pheasant for dinner.

Friday November 6th

Our railhead is now Steenbecque, so we went to Morbecque close by and billeted in the château. The château is not half so nice as we thought it would be, as it is unfurnished and the people are not very affable. Lunched with Niecy and Rose his gunner, who seems sensible. Kicked a football about this afternoon and then dined with Bottles and had a good dinner.

Met a bloke called Grant (Scottie), special enlistment, was in the Gurkhas, who has done very good work spy hunting and has caught several.

Saturday November 7th

Chose lorries for No.1 Section and Anderson chose for No.2. Went into G.H.Q. to get a pass to Amiens. Had lunch in the pub here and then at 3.0 p.m. started for Amiens in the car, a lorry full of artificers having started earlier. Arrived at Amiens at 6.0 p.m., and Turner and I got a billet at the Hôtel de Commerce. Had dinner with Gaby and bought some gloves and maps. Went to bed early. It was a great luxury sleeping in a bed again, as I had not slept in one since Aulnoye on August 24th.

Sunday November 8th

Went off at 8.30 a.m. and found nearly all the lorries had been put on rail by the French, so there were very few spares left. Went down to the railway station but could not find the lorries put on rail. Went to Talmas and found the lorry there and the men well at work on the one that had fallen down. We had to remove a tree, take the engine out and then upset the chassis. Jackson, a special reserve second lieutenant, rolled up after lunch as he was ordered to collect this lorry, but I told him it was ours by Gilpin's order.

At 3.0 p.m. took the lorry and a couple of men into Amiens and collected a two ton Hallford back wheel and springs. When I got back I found the lorry dismantled, so I went back to Amiens and the mist was so bad that I could not see the sides of the road. I met Jackson then and we dined together. Colonel Fitzwilliams had been blowing around Amiens, but I missed him.

Monday November 9th

Went down to the station and got a couple of springs and then had a bath at the Hôtel Belfast. I then went to Talmas and saw the various parts placed on the lorry, had lunch and came back. The lorry left at 1.30 p.m. and I left at 1.50 and arrived here at 5.40, having had a very good trip up. At a small pub where I lunched a girl and a dog were feeding off the same plate.

Tuesday November 10th

Cheeroh! Me. Châhop! [*Today was E.S.H.'s birthday. He was twenty-seven.*] Had a rotten night as I once more took to my couch of ammunition boxes instead of a feather bed. Took rifle inspection and then squad drill for the lance corporals. Went to the railway station and posted letters and got some cotton waste. Helped an R.G.A. [*Royal Garrison Artillery*] Foden lorry out of the ditch. Ate bully twice. Anderson built a card castle one pack high. Received the *Weekly Times* and *Advertiser*.

Wednesday November 11th

Beastly day and a real November one. Anderson went up with ammunition. Went to the station in the Vauxhall and got a Thorney petrol tank from Perry to replace the one on my Albion. After lunch Gibbon and Pom arrived back from Paris and Rouen. The farmer who owns this place behaves in rather a suspicious manner and is always out all night and loiters around our lorries and we suspect him of being a spy. Today we discovered quite by accident a wire came into his château through one of the windows, so Goldsmith and I went into G.H.Q. at St Omer to tell the Intelligence Corps.

They gave us tea and dinner and are a rum crowd and very mixed and we had an amusing evening. Some of them are very nice. We brought back a Scotland Yard 'teck' disguised as a soldier servant, who is going to investigate. A very stormy wet day.

Intelligence Corps

It was not until 1905, shortly after the Boer War, that specific recommendations were made for the formation of an Intelligence Corps, despite the timeless need for intelligence throughout history. Thus in 1914 the Intelligence Corps began to develop its skills during World War I, including the use of air photographs, counter intelligence and methods of interrogation. Despite many successes the Corps planners decided intelligence was required only during times of war and the Corps was disbanded at the end of the War. It was not re-formed until the outbreak of the Second World War.

Thursday November 12th

Got up and had breakfast at 8.0 a.m. Went for a ride with Gilpin on one of his horses. The beast put me on his neck as soon as we started, and then I put him over a small gate, which he took very well after a few refusals.

We had a nice ride through Steenbecque and the woods south of here and it was a lovely day. Was not very hungry and ate a very small lunch, after which

Anderson, Pot and I went to St Omer. Had tea with Ditmas. Got some money from Morrison as I paid some of his men the day we went to Amiens.

Laird says he has seen the list and that I am going home to train Kitchener's army in three weeks time. Got back here at 7.30 p.m. and then had to go out to Ebblinghem to inspect a lorry which was ditched. Bray had reported it was impossible to get it out, but he is an incompetent B.F. and it could be got out in an hour by working.

> ### Kitchener's Army
>
> *Britain was totally unprepared for a war on the scale of World War I, with no real reserves of manpower or equipment and only a small munitions industry. Its army was a very fine one, but it was not designed for a war of this magnitude, and by the end of 1914 the horrendous casualties of the preceding months (nearly 90,000 killed, wounded or missing) had reduced it to a vestige of its former self. Kitchener had no problem in recruiting volunteers for his 'New Army', but volunteers take time to train and equip, and it was not until 1916 that they were ready to take the field in effective numbers. Meanwhile those regulars who had survived the early battles were an important resource when it came to training the new recruits.*

Friday November 13th

The lorry was extracted from the ditch in under an hour this morning. Rotten day and beastly wet. A new fellow joined yesterday and he is Glasgow Scotch.

Went to the station and found two rear Halley wheels have come back retyred, so they are going to Ebblinghem to fit. Those of the Halley at Renescure are lost. Had a good lunch at the pub. The Ebblinghem lorry filled up with barbed wire and returned here.

Received one letter from Mum and three from Kinker and a parcel and letter from Mum. [*Kinker was E.S.H's older brother, Kendall*] A very wet night.

Saturday November 14th

At 8.30 a.m. I took a lorry up to the 23rd Brigade at Neuve-Eglise (*Flemish Nieuwkerke*), as they wanted some barbed wire. The roads were awful, but everything was quiet except for gunfire. I then went to Steenwerck to see Bearne re some tyres and back wheels. A very wet and stormy day. Lunched in the pub and kicked a footer about afterwards. Received a letter from Marjorie. [*The Editor does not know who Marjorie is*]

The 'teck' left today and the old man is not a spy, but has had a row with his wife and wanders about at night and is rather doleful.

> ## Battle of Ypres—The Final Phase
>
> *The Germans made one last attempt to break the Allied line on November 10th-11th. In the British sector the main thrust was north and south of the Menin Road against the 1st and 2nd Divisions and a division formed from scratch units of II Corps under Major-General F.D.W.Wing. Later it became known as the Battle of Nonne Böschen (Nun's Wood) and it was a close run thing, with the German forces, which included units of the crack Prussian Guard, breaking through the British line in places. But by dark the line had been restored, and thereafter with the onset of winter things quietened down.*

Sunday November 15th

A very raw nasty wet windy stormy cold day, and got up in a very bad temper. Went down to the station and got very wet. Gottwaltz and Anderson went to St Omer.

Despatched two sets of Hallford wheels to Paris to be re-tyred. Morrison came in before lunch.

Monday November 16th

Beastly wet and went to the station. In the afternoon I went to look for the paymaster and had to go up to Dranouter. The Germans were shelling a hill close by. 'Black marias' were bursting on it pretty frequently.

The paymaster was not here, so I went through Neuve-Eglise to la Crèche, but missed him. Came back very cold and found we had run out of coal so went to bed early.

Tuesday November 17th

Again very wet. Did company work in the morning and went to look for the paymaster in the afternoon. Found him and touched him for £5. Then went and saw Bearne and came back via Hazebrouck.

Got a puncture and met 1st Division who are coming back to rest. Received two parcels from Mum and a letter from Kath.

Wednesday November 18th

Froze like blazes last night and there was ice everywhere. Dressed very quickly. Went to the station. After lunch Gottwaltz and I went to St Omer. Saw Wilder, Branden and Smith. Came back via Hazebrouck. Saw Morrison. Quite cold. Had tea with Ditmus. Saw list and I am for home. Roast beef dinner—good.

Thursday November 19th

A very cold morning but it did not freeze so much. Moved at 10.0 a.m. to Hazebrouck, our new railhead. Very difficult to find a billet as 1st Corps is here, but eventually got an empty house. Snowed all day, pretty heavily. Met Major Purchas of the 24th at the railway station [*24 Company A.S.C. was a Horse Transport Company attached to the 6th Division*]. He is R.T.O. [*Railway Transport Officer*] and used to be my skipper in South Africa. It had stopped snowing when we went to bed and there were about four inches of snow.

Friday November 20th

Got up at 7.0 a.m. It was very cold and freezing hard and we had about ten degrees of frost during the night. At about 10.0 a.m. a German aeroplane dropped three bombs a hundred yards from here, fatally wounding a French civy and making fair holes and breaking all the windows. It returned later and dropped three more, but these fell in a field. It was very cold all day but nice and sunny. Had lunch at the railway station and had a long talk with Purchas. Several lorries froze up. Received two lorries (Karriers) of fifteen pounder ammunition for Warwickshire R.H.A.T. Ate half a pheasant for dinner.

Warwickshire R.H.A. Territorial Battery

Originally raised by Lord Brooke at Warwick Castle, this unit was allocated as artillery support to the 1st South Midland Mounted Brigade. The battery was duplicated in 1914 forming 1/1st and 2/1st Warwickshire Batteries. The 1/1st was the first Territorial artillery unit to go overseas on active service spending the whole war in France. Note the reference to '15 pounder ammunition'. In order to equip some units with guns, the army was forced to use several types of artillery weapon in addition to standard models. The ammunition referred to here was probably for the 15 pounder QF gun, which was made in Germany in the late 1800's and 1900. Some Territorial batteries moved to France with this weapon, and several saw action. It was replaced in 1915.

Saturday November 21st

Again a very heavy frost and trouble in starting engines. One cracked cylinder, one frozen pump and a broken water jacket. Damn cold. Went up to the station and saw Morrison and Spafford. 1st Corps arrived today to rest. Gibbon is spending twenty-four hours in the trenches. Received a letter from old Shortland.

Sunday November 22nd

Bray has gone off on ten days leave to look for his kit. Morrison brought down the 'Unie Car'. Pom and I took the Sunbeam to Arcques and fetched 1,000 sandbags, which weighed down the car, so we had to come back slowly. Called in at Renescure and found the Halley assembled, but with the water jacket of one cylinder cracked. Very difficult traveling after dark as the roads and fields are white and there are no hedges. Frost nails. Very cold tonight and ice.

German aeroplanes have taken to dropping 'arrows'. Would much rather have bombs. Gibbon returned tonight safely. One of our oil pumps froze tonight and so did a petrol pipe. Roads all ice and very slippery.

Arrows

These were a French invention and were steel darts, about the size of a pen, pointed at one end with steel feathers. They were kept in a box about the size of a petrol can, and were released by pulling the bottom out. After release they spread wide. The Germans soon copied them, but they were quite quickly discontinued. One of their more unfortunate characteristics was that they were often contaminated by the oil in which they were kept, leading to infected wounds in those unlucky enough to be struck by them.

Monday November 23rd

Went and saw Robinson and Archibald to borrow a man to acetylene weld. Saw Swabey who is now a Lieutenant Colonel. Drove the Unie and took quite a long time to get into it.

Goldsmith went off to see about leave and Pom and I went to Renescure and fetched a cylinder from the Halley. The Germans have 176 railway trains empty here waiting to take back two corps if the Russians win another battle, and we have ? aeroplanes ready to drop bombs on them when they become loaded. Thawed tonight.

Tuesday November 24th

Received a *Weekly Times*, parcel and postcard from Mother. Heard of a French process for temporarily mending cracked cylinders. Fill with copper and solder. Went into Renescure and St Omer and made arrangements for oxy-acetylene process on our cylinders tomorrow.

The Indian troops mined two miles of their trenches, retired out of them and then, when the Germans had reoccupied them, they blew up the lot. Some of our cavalry had to occupy a trench in which dead Germans and French had been buried, and one man thought he was standing on a mangle, but discovered it was a German's head and was promptly sick. Hand grenade (squeaker).

The Eastern Front
[See opposite]

As already mentioned the Germans hoped to dispose of France first and then deal with Russia later, thus avoiding a war on two fronts. So they left only a holding force of four and a half corps, one cavalry division, garrison troops in Königsburg and some territorial brigades to defend East Prussia against a Russian invasion. The plan depended on the slowness with which the Russians could mobilize, estimated at around six weeks, but in fact they were ready much sooner and the Russian 1st Army crossed the frontier on August 17th. It was to be the northern claw of a pincer movement (with the Russian 2nd Army coming up from the south) designed to entrap the German forces.

The Russian 1st Army scored a partial success against the Germans on August 20th at Gumbinnen, but failed to follow it up, thus allowing them a breathing space to re-organize. However the psychological effect on the German nation was considerable. East Prussia had a symbolic importance as the home of the Teutonic Knights and the Junkers, with Königsburg as the city where the first Hohenzollern sovereign had been crowned King of Prussia in 1701. Added to this was the fear of invasion, fuelled by the folk memory of Slavic hordes from the East ('the Cossacks are coming').

The immediate result was the dismissal of the two most senior generals in the East and their replacement by Ludendorff (the hero of Liège) as Chief of Staff, with General von Hindenburg (called out of retirement) to be Commander in Chief. A second result was the decision by von Moltke to despatch two corps and a cavalry division from the Western front as reinforcements, thus further eroding the Schlieffen Plan. They arrived too late to affect the Battle of Tanneburg, when on August 26th-30th Ludendorff virtually destroyed the Russian 2nd Army. He then turned his attention to the Russian 1st Army, and in the Battle of the Masurian Lakes (September 9th-10th) drove the Russians back across the frontier with the loss of 125,000 of their men.

Meanwhile further south it was the Russians who were victorious. In a series of engagements (August 26th to September 10th) culminating in the Battle of Lemberg they inflicted a defeat on the Austro-Hungarian army from which it never recovered. The Austrians suffered 250,000 casualties with a further 100,000 taken prisoner. Later (October 17th to November 10th) the Russians advanced through Poland on Silesia, but were halted by the German 9th Army at the Battle of Lodz (November 18th-25th).

Wednesday November 25th

Started with Pom at 10.0 a.m. for St Omer with two cracked cylinders, and picked up two French experts in oxy-acetylene process at Renescure. Went to St Omer and found that there was no oxygen, so returned to Renescure and mended cylinders by filling with tin.

Chip out crack in water jacket and clean and rub with copper, then apply sal ammoniac and then fill with tin with soldering iron. If lorries won't start in the morning inject boiling petrol. Bray came back last night. Reported to Wilder and heard officially that I was for home on December 6th. Received letter from Mum and Tapy.

Thursday November 26th

Goldsmith and Gottwaltz went off on leave at 6.0 a.m. this morning and caught the 10.0 a.m. boat at Calais. Saw an article in the *Telegraph* for an increase of pay which reduces mine by 1/- a day. After lunch Pom and I went up to the H.Q. of 5th Cavalry Brigade to see the paymaster, but he was not there. Morrison dined with us and we had roast pheasants for dinner.

Friday November 27th

Went up to the field cashier at 8.30 a.m. and drew 1,000 francs from the cashier. Drove Burton back. A glorious morning but a heavy storm later. Anderson and Nesbitt went into G.H.Q. Sergeant Major, Q.M.S., Mortlock, Honeybourne and Bernadin went on 72 hours leave. Had a very good joint of roast mutton for dinner. Received an order from A.A. and Q.M.G. to move to Vieux Berquin.

Saturday November 28th

Went to Vieux Berquin with Gibbon at 8.30 a.m. to look for a parking ground, but could find none suitable except in the square in our old place. Got a good billet and borrowed the interpreter from the Column. Moved at 2.0 p.m. and arrived at 4.0 p.m.

Renescure Halley came in and cylinder is holding well. They have a re-tyring plant on rail at Strazeele. Had a good curry for dinner. Went into G.H.Q. this evening to see Wilder. A filthy night and raining very heavily and eggs were 3c each. Got bogged. The old woman has pegged out and was buried today.

Sunday November 29th

Had trouble about Anderson's billet, but squared it. Went to Hazebrouck and went through papers. Davies came into lunch and was very doleful.

Received fifty cigarettes from Aunt Kitty and a parcel from Mum. [*The Editor is not sure where Aunt Kitty comes in the family—according to one source a courtesy aunt, possibly a cousin on E.S.H.'s mother's side.*] Randall came back with the Vauxhall at 7.30 p.m. Gibbon went off at 7.0 p.m. for Calais on leave.

Monday November 30th

Went home.

Appendices

Appendix 1: Order of Battle—August 1914   82

Appendix 2: Order of Battle—November 1914   85

Appendix 3: Army Colleagues and Acquaintances   91

Appendix 4: Extracts from the Corps Journal   99

Appendix 5: 'Old Bill'   108

Appendix 6: E.S.H.'s Army Records—Relevant Entries   109

Appendix 7: Resources   113

Appendix 1
Order of Battle—August 1914

General Headquarters

Commander-in-Chief: Field-Marshal Sir J.D.P.French, G.C.B., G.C.V.O., K.C.M.G.
Chief of the General Staff: Lieut-Gen. Sir A.J.Murray, K.C.B., C.V.O., D.S.O.
Major General, General Staff: Maj-Gen. H.H.Wilson, C.B., D.S.O.
Quartermaster-General: Maj-Gen. Sir W.R.Robertson, K.C.V.O., C.B., D.S.O.

The Cavalry Division
G.O.C.: Maj-Gen. E.H.Allenby, C.B.

1st Cavalry Brigade
G.O.C.: Brig-Gen. C.J.Briggs C.B.
2nd Dragoon Guards (Queen's Bays); 5th (Princess Charlotte of Wales's) Dragoon Guards; 11th (Prince Albert's Own) Hussars; 1st Signal Troop.

2nd Cavalry Brigade
G.O.C.: Brig-Gen. H. de B. de Lisle C.B., D.S.O.
4th (Royal Irish) Dragoon Guards; 9th (Queen's Royal) Lancers; 18th (Queen Mary's Own) Hussars; 2nd Signal Troop.

3rd Cavalry Brigade
G.O.C.: Brig-Gen. H. de la P. Gough C.B.
4th (Queen's Own) Hussars; 5th (Royal Irish) Lancers; 16th (The Queen's) Lancers; 3rd Signal Troop.

4th Cavalry Brigade
G.O.C.: Brig-Gen. Hon. C.E.Bingham C.V.O., C.B.
Composite Regt of Household Cavalry (1st & 2nd Life Guards & Royal Horse Guards); 6th Dragoon Guards (Carabiniers); 3rd (King's Own) Hussars; 4th Signal Troop.

Cavalry Divisional Troops
III & VII Brigades R.H.A. with Ammunition Columns; 1st Field Squadron R.E.; 1st Signal Squadron; H.Q. 1st Cavalry Division A.S.C.; 1st, 2nd, 3rd & 4th Cavalry Field Ambulances.

5th Cavalry Brigade (independent Command)
G.O.C.: Brig-Gen. Sir P.W.Chetwode, Bart., D.S.O.

2nd Dragoons (Royal Scots Greys); 12th (Prince of Wales's Royal) Lancers; 20th Hussars; J Battery R.H.A. and Ammunition Column; 4th Field Troop R.E.; 5th Signal Troop; 5th Cavalry Field Ambulance.

I Corps

G.O.C.: Lieut-Gen. Sir D.Haig, K.C.B., K.C.I.E., K.C.V.O., A.D.C-Gen.
Brig-Gen.G.S.: Brig-Gen. J.E.Gough, V.C., C.M.G., A.D.C.

1st Division
G.O.C.: Maj-Gen. S.H.Lomax

1st (Guards) Brigade
G.O.C.: Brig-Gen. F.I.Maxse, C.V.O., C.B., D.S.O.
1st Coldstream Guards; 1st Scots Guards (Royal Highlanders); 1st Black Watch; 2nd Royal Munster Fusiliers.

2nd Infantry Brigade
G.O.C.: Brig-Gen. E.S.Bulfin, C.V.O., C.B.
2nd Royal Sussex Regiment; 1st Loyal North Lancashire Regiment; 1st Northamptonshire Regiment; 2nd The King's Royal Rifle Corps.

3rd Infantry Brigade
G.O.C.: Brig-Gen. H.A.S.Landon, C.B.
1st The Queen's (Royal West Surrey Regiment); 1st The South Wales Borderers; 1st The Gloucestershire Regiment; 2nd The Welch Regiment.

Divisional Troops
C Squadron, 15th (The King's Hussars); 1st Cyclist Company;
XXV, XXVI, XXXIX & XLIII (Howitzer) Brigades with Ammunition Columns R.F.A.; 20th Heavy Battery R.G.A. and Heavy Battery Ammunition Column; 1st Divisional Ammunition Column; 23rd & 26th Field Companies R.E.; 1st Signal Company; 1st Divisional Train A.S.C.; 1st, 2nd & 3rd Field Ambulances.

2nd Division
G.O.C.: Maj-Gen. C.C.Monro, C.B.

4th (Guards) Brigade
G.O.C.: Brig-Gen. R.Scott-Kerr, C.B., M.V.O., D.S.O.
2nd Grenadier Guards; 2nd Coldstream Guards; 3rd Coldstream Guards; 1st Irish Guards.

5th Infantry Brigade
G.O.C.: Brig-Gen. R.C.B.Haking, C.B.
2nd The Worcestershire Regiment; 2nd the Oxfordshire & Buckinghamshire Light Infantry; 2nd The Highland Light Infantry; 2nd The Connaught Rangers.

6th Infantry Brigade
G.O.C.: Brig-Gen. R.H.Davies, C.B. (New Zealand Staff Corps).
1st The King's (Liverpool Regiment); 2nd The South Staffordshire Regiment; 1st Princess Charlotte of Wales's (Royal Berkshire Regiment); 1st The King's Royal Rifle Corps.

Divisional Troops
B Squadron 15th (The King's) Hussars; 2nd Cyclist Company;
XXXIV, XXXVI, XLI & XLIV (Howitzer) Brigades R.F.A. with Ammunition Columns; 35th Heavy Battery R.G.A. and Heavy Battery Ammunition Column; 2nd Divisional Ammunition Column. 5th & 11th Field Companies R.E.; 2nd Signal Company; 2nd Divisional Train A.S.C.; 4th, 5th & 6th Field Ambulances.

II Corps

G.O.C.: General Sir H.L.Smith-Dorien, G.C.B., D.S.O.
Brig-Gen.G.S.: Brig-Gen. G.T.Forestier-Walker, A.D.C.

3rd Division

G.O.C.: Maj-Gen. H.I.W.Hamilton, C.V.O., C.B., D.S.O.

7th Infantry Brigade
G.O.C.: Brig-Gen. F.W.N.McCracken, C.B., D.S.O.
3rd The Worcestershire Regiment; 2nd The Prince of Wales's Volunteers (South Lancashire Regiment); 1st The Duke of Edinburgh's (Wiltshire Regiment); 2nd The Royal Irish Rifles.

8th Infantry Brigade
G.O.C.: Brig-Gen. B.J.C.Doran, C.B.
2nd The Royal Scots (Lothian Regiment); 2nd The Royal Irish Regiment; 4th The Duke of Cambridge's Own (Middlesex Regiment); 1st The Gordon Highlanders.

9th Infantry Brigade
G.O.C.: Brig-Gen. F.C.Shaw, C.B.
1st The Northumberland Fusiliers; 4th The Royal Fusiliers (City of London Regiment); 1st The Lincolnshire Regiment; 1st The Royal Scots Fusiliers.

Divisional Troops
A Squadron 15th (The King's) Hussars; 3rd Cyclist Company;
XXIII, XL, XLII & XXX (Howitzer) Brigades R.F.A. with Ammunition Columns; 48th Heavy Battery R.G.A. and Heavy Battery Ammunition Column; 3rd Divisional Ammunition Column;
56th & 57th Field Companies R.E.; 3rd Signal Company; 3rd Divisional Train A.S.C.; 7th, 8th & 9th Field Ambulances.

5th Division

G.O.C.: Maj-Gen. Sir C.Ferguson, Bart., C.B., M.V.O., D.S.O.

13th Infantry Brigade
G.O.C.: Brig-Gen. G.J.Cuthbert, C.B.
2nd The King's Own Scottish Borderers; 2nd The Duke of Wellington's (West Riding Regiment); 1st The Queen's Own (Royal West Kent Regiment); 2nd The King's Own (Yorkshire Light Infantry).

14th Infantry Brigade
G.O.C.: Brig-Gen. S.P.Rolt, C.B.
2nd The Suffolk Regiment; 1st The East Surrey Regiment; 1st The Duke of Cornwall's Light Infantry; 2nd The Manchester Regiment.

15th Infantry Brigade
G.O.C.: Brig-Gen. A.E.W. Count Gleichen, K.C.V.O., C.B., C.M.G., D.S.O. Eq.
1st The Norfolk Regiment; 1st The Bedfordshire Regiment; 1st The Cheshire Regiment; 1st The Dorsetshire Regiment.

Divisional Troops
A Squadron 19th (Queen Alexandra's Own Royal) Hussars; 5th Cyclist Company.
XV, XXVII, XXVIII & VIII (Howitzer) Brigades R.F.A. with Ammunition Columns; 108th Heavy Battery R.G.A. and Heavy Battery Ammunition Column.
17th & 59th Field Companies R.E.; 5th Signal Company; 5th Divisional Train A.S.C.; 13th, 14th & 15th Field Ambulances.

Appendix 2
Order of Battle—November 1914

I & II Corps

As in **Appendix 1**, apart from the following changes

I Corps
  1st Division
    1st (Guards) Brigade: The 1st Cameron Highlanders *replaced* The 2nd Royal Munster Fusiliers; 14th London Regiment (London Scottish) *added*.
  2nd Division
    4th (Guards Brigade): 1st Hertfordshire Regiment *added*.
    5th Infantry Brigade: 9th Highland Light Infantry *added*.

II Corps
  3rd Division: *G.O.C.*: Maj-Gen. F.D.V.Wing, C.B. *replaced previous G.O.C.*
    8th Infantry Brigade: The Devonshire Regiment *replaced* The 1st Gordon Highlanders; 1st Honourable Artillery Company *added*.
    9th Infantry Brigade: 10th The King's (Liverpool Regiment) *added*.
  5th Division
    13th Infantry Brigade: 1/9th London Regiment (Queen Victoria's Rifles) *added*.

III Corps

G.O.C.: Maj-Gen. W.P.Pulteney, C.B., D.S.O.
Brig-Gen.G.S.: Brig-Gen. J.P. Du Cane, C.B.

4th Division

G.O.C.: Maj-Gen. H.F.M.Wilson, C.B.

10th Infantry Brigade
G.O.C.: Brig-Gen. J.A.L.Haldane, C.B., D.S.O.
1st The Royal Warwickshire Regiment; 2nd Seaforth Highlanders (Ross-shire Buffs, The Duke of Albany's); 1st Princess Victoria's (Royal Irish Fusiliers); 2nd The Royal Dublin Fusiliers.

11th Infantry Brigade
G.O.C.: Brig-Gen. A.G.Hunter-Weston, C.B., D.S.O.
1st Prince Albert's (Somerset Light Infantry); 1st The East Lancashire Regiment; 1st The Hampshire Regiment; 1st The Rifle Brigade (Prince Consort's Own); 1/5th London Regiment (London Rifle Brigade).

12th Infantry Brigade
G.O.C.: Brig-Gen. H.F.M.Wilson, C.B.
1st King's Own (Royal Lancashire Regiment); 2nd The Lancashire Fusiliers; 2nd The Royal Inskilling Fusiliers; 2nd The Essex Regiment.

Divisional Troops
B Squadron 19th (Queen Alexandra's Own) Hussars; 4th Cyclist Company.
XIV, XXIX, XXXII & XXXVII (Howitzer) Brigades R.F.A. with Ammunition Columns; 31st Heavy Battery R.G.A. and Heavy Battery Ammunition Column; 4th Divisional Ammunition Column.
7th & 9th Field Companies R.E.; 4th Signal Company; 4th Divisional Train A.S.C.; 10th, 11th & 12th Field Ambulances.

6th Division
G.O.C.: Maj-Gen. J.L.Kerr, C.B.

16th Infantry Brigade
G.O.C.: Brig-Gen. E.C.Ingouville-Williams, C.B., D.S.O.
1st The Buffs (East Kent Regiment); 1st The Leicestershire Regiment; 1st The King's (Shropshire Light Infantry); 2nd The York and Lancaster Regiment.

17th Infantry Brigade
G.O.C.: Brig-Gen. W.R.B.Doran, C.B., D.S.O.
1st The Royal Fusiliers (City of London Regiment); 1st The Prince of Wales (North Staffordshire Regiment); 2nd The Prince of Wales Leinster Regiment (Royal Canadians); 3rd The Rifle Brigade (The Prince Consort's Own).

18th Infantry Brigade
G.O.C.: Brig-Gen. W.N.Congreve, V.C., C.B., M.V.O.
1st The Prince of Wales's Own (West Yorkshire Regiment); 1st The East Yorkshire Regiment; 2nd The Sherwood Foresters (Nottinghamshire & Derbyshire Regiment); 2nd The Durham Light Infantry; 1/16th London Regiment (Queen's Westminster Rifles).

19th Infantry Brigade
2nd Royal Welch Fusiliers; 2nd The Cameronians (Scottish Rifles); 1st Middlesex Regiment; 2nd Argyll & Sutherland Highlanders; 1/5th The Cameronians (Scottish Rifles).

Divisional Troops
C Squadron 19th (Queen Alexandra's Own) Hussars; 6th Cyclist Company.
II, XXIV, XXXVIII & XII (Howitzer) Brigades R.F.A. with Ammunition Columns; 24th Heavy Battery R.G.A. and Heavy Battery Ammunition Column.
12th & 38th Field Companies R.E.; 6th Signal Company; 6th Divisional Train A.S.C.; 16th, 17th & 18th Field Ambulance.

Cavalry Corps
G.O.C.: Lieut -Gen. E.H.H.Allenby, C.B.
Colonel, G.S.: Brig-Gen. G. de S. Barrow.

1st Cavalry Division
G.O.C.: Maj-Gen. H. de B. de Lisle, C.B., D.S.O.

1st Cavalry Brigade
G.O.C.: Brig-Gen. C.J.Briggs C.B.
2nd Dragoon Guards (The Queen's Bays); 5th (Princess Charlotte of Wales's) Dragoon Guards; 11th (Prince Albert's Own) Hussars; 1st Signal Troop.

2nd Cavalry Brigade
G.O.C.: Brig-Gen. R.L.Mullens.
4th (Royal Irish) Dragoon Guards; 9th (Queen's Royal) Lancers; 18th (Queen Mary's Own) Hussars; 2nd Signal Troop.

Divisional Troops
VII Brigade R.H.A. with Ammunition Column.
1st Field Squadron R.E.; 1st Signal Column; 1st Cavalry Divisional Supply Column A.S.C.; 1st & 3rd Cavalry Field Ambulances.

2nd Cavalry Division
G.O.C.: Maj-Gen. H. de la P. Gough, C.B.

3rd Cavalry Brigade
G.O.C.: Brig-Gen. J.Vaughan, D.S.O.
4th (Queen's Own) Hussars; 5th (Royal Irish) Lancers; 16th (The Queen's) Lancers; 3rd Signal Troop.

4th Cavalry Brigade
G.O.C.: Brig-Gen. Hon. C.E.Bingham, C.V.O., C.B.
The (Queen's Own) Oxfordshire Hussars; 6th Dragoon Guards (Carabiniers); 3rd (King's Own) Hussars; 4th Signal Troop.

5th Cavalry Brigade
G.O.C.: Brig-Gen. Sir P.W.Chetwode, Bart., D.S.O.
2nd Dragoons (Royal Scots Greys); 12th (Prince of Wales's Royal) Lancers; 20th Hussars; 5th Signal Troop.

Divisional Troops
III Brigade R.H.A.; 2nd Cavalry Divisional Ammunition Column.
2nd Field Squadron R.E.; 2nd Signal Squadron; 2nd Cavalry Divisional Supply Column A.S.C.; 2nd, 4th & 5th Cavalry Field Ambulances.

3rd Cavalry Division
G.O.C.: Maj-Gen. Hon. J.H.G.Byng, C.B., M.V.O.

6th Cavalry Brigade
G.O.C.: Brig-Gen. E.Makins, D.S.O.
3rd (Prince of Wales's) Dragoon Guards; 1st Royal Dragoons; The North Somerset Yeomanry.

7th Cavalry Brigade
G.O.C.: Brig-Gen. C.T.McM.Kavanagh, C.V.O., C.B., D.S.O.
1st Life Guards; 2nd Life Guards; The Leicestershire Yeomanry.

8th Cavalry Brigade
G.O.C.: Brig-Gen. C.B.Bulkeley-Johnson.
The Royal Horse Guards; 10th (Prince of Wales's Own) Royal Hussars.

Divisional Troops
XV Brigade R.H.A. with Ammunition Column.
3rd Field Squadron R.E.; 3rd Signal Squadron; 3rd Cavalry Divisional Supply Column A.S.C.; 6th & 7th Cavalry Field Ambulances.

IV Corps

G.O.C.: Lieut-Gen. Sir H.S.Rawlinson, Bt, C.V.O, C.B.
Brig-Gen. G.S.: Brig-Gen. R.A.K.Montgomery, C.B., D.S.O.

7th Division

G.O.C.: Maj-Gen. T.Capper, C.B., D.S.O.

20th Brigade
G.O.C.: Brig-Gen. F.J.Heyworth.
1st Grenadier Guards; 2nd Scots Guards; 2nd The Border Regiment; 2nd The Gordon Highlanders.

21st Brigade
G.O.C.: Brig-Gen. H.E.Watts, C.B.
2nd The Bedfordshire Regiment; 2nd The Green Howards (Alexandra, Princess of Wales's Own Yorkshire Regiment); 2nd The Royal Scots Fusiliers; 2nd The Wiltshire Regiment (Duke of Edinburgh's).

22nd Brigade
G.O.C.: Brig-Gen. S.T.B.Lawford.
2nd The Queen's (Royal West Surrey) Regiment; 2nd The Royal Warwickshire Regiment; 1st The Royal Welch Fusiliers; 1st The South Staffordshire Regiment; The 8th Royal Scots.

Divisional Troops
Northumberland Hussars; 7th Cyclist Company.
XIV Brigade R.H.A. with Ammunition Column; XXII & XXXV Brigades R.F.A. with Ammunition Columns; 3rd Heavy Brigade R.G.A. with Ammunition Column; 7th Divisional Ammunition Column.
54th & 55th Field Companies R.E.; 7th Signal Company; 7th Divisional Train A.S.C.; 21st, 22nd & 23rd Field Ambulances.

8th Division

G.O.C.: Maj-Gen. F.J.Davies, C.B.

23rd Brigade
G.O.C.: Brig-Gen. R.J.Pinney
2nd The Devonshire Regiment; 2nd (The Prince of Wales's Own) West Yorkshire Regiment; 2nd The Cameronians (Scottish Rifles); 2nd (The Duke of Cambridge's Own) Middlesex Regiment.

24th Brigade
G.O.C.: Brig-Gen. F.C.Carter, C.B.
1st The Worcestershire Regiment; 2nd The East Lancashire Regiment; 1st The Sherwood Foresters (Nottinghamshire & Derbyshire Regiment); 2nd The Northamptonshire Regiment; 5th Black Watch.

25th Brigade
G.O.C.: Brig-Gen. A.W.G. Lowry Cole, C.B., D.S.O.
2nd The Lincolnshire Regiment; 2nd (Princess Charlotte of Wales's) Royal Berkshire Regiment; 1st The Royal Irish Rifles; 2nd The Rifle Brigade (Prince Consort's Own); The 13th London Regiment (Princess Louise's Kensington Battalion).

Divisional Troops
Northamptonshire Yeomanry; 8th Cyclist Company.
V Brigade R.H.A. with Ammunition Column; XXIII & XLV Brigades R.F.A. with Ammunition Columns; 8th Heavy Brigade R.G.A. with Ammunition Column; 8th Divisional Ammunition Column.
2nd & 15th Field Companies R.E.; 8th Signal Company; 8th Divisional Train A.S.C.; 24th, 25th & 26th Field Ambulances.

Indian Corps
G.O.C.: Lieut-Gen. Sir J.Willcocks, K.C.B., K.C.S.L., K.C.M.G., D.S.O.
Brig-Gen. G.S.: Brig-Gen. H.Hudson, C.B., D.S.O.

The Lahore Division
G.O.C.: Lieut-Gen. H.B.B.Watkis, C.B.

The Ferezepore Brigade
G.O.C.: Brig-Gen. R.G.Egerton, C.B.
1st The Connaught Rangers; 9th Bhopal Infantry; 57th Wilde's Rifles (Frontier Force); 129th Duke of Connaught's Own Baluchis.

The Jullundur Brigade
G.O.C.: Maj-Gen. P.M.Carnegy, C.B.
1st The Manchester Regiment; 15th Ludhiana Sikhs; 47th Sikhs; 59th Scinde Rifles (Frontier Force).

Divisional Troops
15th Lancers (Cureton's Multanis).
V, XL & XVIII Brigades R.F.A. with Ammunition Columns; 109th Heavy Battery R.G.A. with Ammunition Column; Lahore Divisional Ammunition Column.
20th & 21st Companies 3rd Sappers & Miners; Lahore Signal Company; 34th Sikh Pioneers; Lahore Divisional Train; 7th & 8th British Field Ambulances; 111th, 112th & 113th Indian Field Ambulances.

The Meerut Division
G.O.C.: Lieut-Gen. C.A.Anderson, C.B.

The Dehra Dun Brigade
G.O.C.: Brig-Gen. C.E.Johnson.
1st The Seaforth Highlanders (Ross-shire Buffs, The Duke of Albany's); 6th Jat Light Infantry; 2/2nd King Edward's Own Gurkha Rifles (The Sirmoor Rifles); 1/9th Gurkha Rifles.

The Garhwal Brigade
G.O.C.: Maj-Gen. H. D'U. Keary, C.B., D.S.O.
2nd The Leicestershire Regiment; 1/39th Garhwal Rifles; 2/39th Garhwal Rifles; 2/3rd Queen Alexandra's Own Gurkha Rifles.

The Bareilly Brigade
G.O.C.: Maj-Gen. F.Macbean, C.V.O., C.B.
2nd The Black Watch (Royal Highlanders); 41st Dogras; 58th Vaughan's Rifles (Frontier Force); 2/8th Gurkha Rifles.

Divisional Troops
4th Cavalry.
IV, IX & XIII Brigades R.F.A., with Ammunition Columns; 110th Heavy Battery R.G.A. with Ammunition Column; Meerut Divisional Ammunition Column.
3rd & 4th Company 1st King George's Own Sappers & Miners; 107th Pioneers; Meerut Divisional Train; 19th & 20th British Field Ambulances; 128th, 129th & 130th Indian Field Ambulances.

1st Indian Cavalry Division
G.O.C.: Maj-Gen. M.F.Rimington, C.V.O., C.B.

Sialcot Cavalry Brigade
G.O.C.: Brig-Gen. H.P.Leader, C.B.
17th (Duke of Cambridge's Own) Lancers; 6th King Edward's Own Cavalry; 19th Lancers (Fane's Horse); Signal Troop.

Ambala Cavalry Brigade
G.O.C.: Maj-Gen. C.P.W.Pirie.
8th King's Royal Irish Hussars; 9th Hodson's Horse; 30th Lancers (Gordon's Horse); Signal Troop.

Lucknow Cavalry Brigade
G.O.C.: Maj-Gen. G.A.Cookson, C.B.
1st (King's) Dragoon Guards; 29th Lancers (Deccan Horse); 36th Jacob's Horse; Signal Troop.

Divisional Troops
I Indian Brigade R.H.A. with Ammunition Column
2nd Indian Field Troop Engineers; 2nd Indian Signal Squadron; 1st Indian Cavalry Supply Column; Sialcot, Ambala & Lucknow Cavalry Field Ambulances.

Appendix 3
Army Colleagues and Acquaintances

Nearly seventy colleagues and acquaintances are mentioned in the *Diary*, and the Editor has tried, wherever possible, to follow up the names to find out more about them. Also to check the spelling, where an entry is not completely legible. This has involved research into the *Army Lists* and other related documents.

Special attention has been given to those officers who were attached to the same unit as E.S.H., or get more than a passing mention, and some details of their war service and subsequent careers have been included wherever possible. Some others, who have only a brief mention in the *Diary*, have also been included because there are particular points of interest about them—in particular the fact that they trained with E.S.H. or had contact with him during his initial training at Aldershot (the Editor has a received a lot of help here from copies of pages from the *Corps Journal*, which were sent him by the Archivist at the *Royal Logistic Corps Museum*). There are also a number of names in the *Diary* which the Editor has been unable to match with any entries in the *Army Lists*. Some of these may not have been officers (it is not always clear in the *Diary* as to whether or not they were commissioned), and the rest may simply have eluded the Editor in his researches.

Officers attached to 5th Cavalry Brigade Ammunition Park

Goldsmith: George Edward Goldsmith (*born 15 Mar. 1883*) was E.S.H.'s immediate superior, and appears to have been in charge of 5th Cavalry Brigade Ammunition Park. He was commissioned from the Militia into the Cheshire Regiment on 4 Dec. 1901, and transferred to the A.S.C. on 1 Oct. 1903. He was promoted Lieutenant on 4 Dec. 1904 and Captain on 2 Aug. 1911. His war service in France and Belgium was continuous until the Armistice and he was promoted Major on 1 Apr. 1915. He was twice mentioned in despatches and awarded the D.S.O. After the War he was promoted Lieut-Colonel (15 July 1929) and at one time was O.C. R.A.S.C. Northern Ireland District. He retired in the mid-1930's.

Hay: The Editor can find no records that exactly match Captain Hay, Royal Artillery. The two most likely in the *Army List*, Captain E.S. Hay and Captain H.G.F. Hay, are recorded as not having seen war service in France and Belgium until 1915. It is however possible that there is an error in the war service dates for E.S. Hay, and that his arrival in France should be 17 Aug. 1914, not 17 Aug. 1915 (there is a similar mistake in E.S.H.'s record, where his return to France is given as May 1916, instead of May 1915). 17 Aug. 1914 would also correspond with the *Diary* record of 5th Cavalry Brigade Ammunition Park's arrival in France. If this is so Edward Stuart Hay had been a Captain since 26 Sept. 1908, having been commissioned into the Royal Artillery on 7 Mar. 1900. He was promoted Major on 30 Oct. 1914, and finished the War as a Temporary Lieut-Colonel. After the War he continued with his career in the Army and was promoted Lieut-Colonel on 5 Aug. 1923. He retired sometime around 1927.

Gottwaltz: Reginald Lewis Gottwaltz (*born 10 Sept. 1891*) was Captain Hay's successor in charge of the ammunition. He was commissioned on 11 Aug. 1914 into the Royal Artillery. He was promoted Lieutenant on 9 June 1915, Acting Captain on 26 Aug. 1916 and Captain on 3 Nov. 1917. After the War he continued in the Army, with no further promotion, though with a spell as Adjutant in 1919 and as an Adjutant T.A. from 1922-8. He left the Army early in 1929.

Anderson: R.W. or A.C.M.—There are two possible candidates for the officer mentioned in the *Diary*, that is assuming the policy was to send officers with temporary commissions to France immediately after being commissioned. R.W.Anderson was commissioned as a Temporary 2nd Lieutenant into the A.S.C. on 24 Oct. 1914. He was discharged from the army in 1919 having reached the rank of Temporary Major. A.C.M.Anderson was commissioned as a Temporary 2nd Lieutenant into the A.S.C. on 20 Oct. 1914. He also reached the rank of Temporary Major and was discharged in 1919.

Bray: N. James Edward Bray was a private in the A.S.C. with 1st Ammunition Park, who was commissioned as a 2nd Lieutenant on 24 Oct. 1914. A number of skilled drivers and mechanics were persuaded to volunteer for war service, and some of these were commissioned. He was probably one of them. He disappears from the Army Lists in mid-1915. According to the *Medal Roll* he transferred to the Royal Navy Marines Battalion Reserve where he is listed as a Chief Motor Mechanic.

Gibbon: The *Diary* entry for Oct.26 reads: 'Gibbon arrived to take over the Park', and his name appears regularly in the remaining few weeks. However there is no A.S.C. officer of that name in the *Army Lists* for that period, so who he was remains a mystery. It is just possible that the *Diary* entry refers to the taking over of the ammunition, in which case a certain Capt. J.H.Gibbon is the only possibility. He had a distinguished career, ending up as a full Colonel and Garrison Commander at Woolwich and Commandant of the R.A. Depot there in the mid-1930's. But Gottwaltz seems to have remained with the Park, which makes this suggestion unlikely.

Colleagues with particular mentions

'Tapy': Emerson Collis Pinder (*born 3 Sept. 1889*) is the only one of E.S.H.'s colleagues mentioned in the *Diary* who was known personally to the Editor. In fact he was a guest at the latter's wedding in 1969, having been a long-standing friend of E.S.H. through the years. He was commissioned into the Dorset Regiment on 18 Sept. 1909, and transferred to the A.S.C. on 2 Oct. 1911 (the same date as E.S.H.'s transfer). He was on the same *Junior Officers' Course* at Aldershot as E.S.H. (1911-13), and also on the same *Long M.T. Course* (1913-14). He was made a Temporary Captain at the same time as E.S.H. on 30 Nov. 1914, but unlike him did not return home for any length of time at that point. During World War I he was awarded the M.C. and bar and mentioned in despatches. Later he was promoted Major on 5 Jan.1929 and Lieut-Colonel on 28 Apr. 1936 and was a Chief Instructor at the *R.A.S.C. Training Centre* from 1931-4. He was promoted Colonel just before the outbreak of World War II on 28 Aug. 1939 and Acting Brigadier on 22 May 1942. He retired from the Army at the end of 1944 or beginning of 1945. The Editor remembers him as a somewhat eccentric retired officer who still rode a motorbike in his early sixties. (*See Diary entries for Sept.6, Oct.1, 28, Nov.25*)

Allden: Stanley Guy Allden (*born 14 Aug. 1888*) played in the same hockey team as E.S.H. in 1912, though he seems to have completed his training by then, having been commissioned into the A.S.C. on 19 Sept. 1908. He was promoted Captain on 30 Oct. 1914 and Temporary Major on 30 Nov. 1914. He is listed as a Lieut-Colonel with the Reserve in the Army List for March 1923. (*See Diary entries for Sept.8 & 12*)

Archibald: Gordon King Archibald (*born 12 May 1985*) was another hockey player who was in the same team as E.S.H. in 1912. He was commissioned into the A.S.C. on 22 Nov. 1905. During World War I he saw service in France and Belgium and then from May 1916 onwards in Mesopotamia and was twice mentioned in despatches. After the War he continued in the R.A.S.C. and by 1940 had reached the rank of Brigadier and was Assistant Director of Supplies and Transport Eastern Command. He seems to have had contact with E.S.H. occasionally down the years, chiefly in connection with golf, playing in the same golf meetings in 1927 and 1934. (*See Diary entry for Nov.23*)

Bearne: Lewis Collinswood Bearne (*born 8 Sept. 1983*) is of interest in that E.S.H. obviously knew him from some earlier time, as he states that he had no idea he was in the A.S.C. (*see Diary entry for Aug.21*). In fact, although he was commissioned into the Duke of Cornwall's Light Infantry on 27 Jul. 1901, he was attached to the A.S.C. in the South African War and transferred to the A.S.C. on 1 Oct. 1902. During World War I he saw service in France and Belgium and later in the Balkans. While serving in Serbia in October 1916 he crawled under a lorry, which had caught on fire and which was loaded with bombs, and put the fire out, for which he was later awarded the Albert medal for gallantry. He ended his career in the mid-1920's as a Lieut-Colonel. (*See Diary entries for Aug.21, Nov.14 & 17*)

Bell: Joseph Anthony Douglas Bell (*born 23 Jul. 1982*) appears with E.S.H. in the photo of the tennis players on page 95. He was commissioned into the Royal Artillery on 19 Dec. 1900. After a time in the Indian Army, he transferred as a Captain to the A.S.C. on 18 Nov. 1910. He was taken prisoner (along with Lieut. L.G. Humphries) during the retreat from Mons. He retired from the Army as a Major in 1924. (*See Diary entry for Sept.3*)

'Bertie': *Probably* Eric Bertram Rowcroft (*born 28 Jan. 1921*). He was a year behind E.S.H. in his training, but they would have overlapped at Aldershot. He was commissioned into the A.S.C. on 9 Sept. 1911 and went to France as a 2nd Lieutenant in August 1914. He was promoted Lieutenant on 9 Sept. 1914, Temporary Captain on 30 Nov. 1914 and Acting Major on 30 Mar. 1917. His war service was mostly in France and Belgium and he was twice mentioned in despatches. In Jan. 1918 he went to the *War Office* as a Staff Captain, where he remained until Jan. 1922. He was an Instructor at the *R.A.S.C. Training Establishment* in Aldershot in the 1920's and would have overlapped with E.S.H. there. In 1936 he had a brief spell as O.C. R.A.S.C. in Palestine and Trans-Jordan and was promoted Lieut-Colonel on 9 Mar. 1938. In World War II he was at the *War Office* as a Brigadier at the same time as E.S.H., and was Deputy Director of Supplies and Transport. (*See Diary entry for Oct.7*)

Brooke-Murray: Kenneth Algernon Brooke-Murray (*born 8 Mar. 1992*) was another who was a year behind E.S.H. in his training at Aldershot. He was commissioned into the A.S.C. on 9 Sept 1911, and was a Staff Captain by 1915 and Acting Military Landing Officer. He transferred to the Royal Flying Corps in Aug. 1916. (*See Diary entry for Oct.13*)

Caulfeild: James Crosby Caulfeild (*spelt 'Caulfield' in the Diary*) (*born 21 Feb. 1892*) was also a year behind E.S.H. in his training at Aldershot, having been commissioned into the A.S.C. on 9 Sept. 1911. When E.S.H. met him at St Quentin he was still in the A.S.C, but in October 1914 he transferred at his own request to the infantry, joining the 2nd Battalion of the Manchester Regiment as a Lieutenant. He was killed in action near Wulverghem on 18 Nov. 1914 while in command of C Company. (*See Diary entry for Aug.27*)

Clarke: Wilfred Herbert Clarke (*born 13 Feb. 1892*) was six months behind E.S.H. as an A.S.C. officer, having been commissioned into the A.S.C. on 7 Feb. 1912, but they overlapped at

Aldershot. He continued in the A.S.C. after the War and was a Lieut-Colonel and Assistant Director of Supplies and Transport in East Africa at the beginning of World War II. (*See Diary entries for Sept.13 & Oct.1*)

Courteney: Hugh Aldred Courtenay (*born 5 Nov. 1892*) is another that E.S.H. would have met at Aldershot (in fact he is pictured standing in the same row as E.S.H. in the photo on page 95). He was commissioned into the A.S.C. on 7 Feb. 1912 and promoted Lieutenant on 5 Aug. 1914. In 1917 he transferred as a Captain into the Royal Flying Corps. (*See Diary entry for Oct.8*)

Ditmas: F.I.L.Ditmus was a Railway Transport Officer (*See entry for Major Purchas for details of what this involved*) and seems to have been based at St Omer. He was made a Lieutenant on 5 Aug. 1914 but graded as Staff Captain. (*See Diary entries for Oct.16, Nov.3,12 & 18*)

'Fitz': Probably Edward Herbert Fitzherbert (*born 5 Dec. 1985*). He was at Aldershot at the same time as E.S.H. and in the same hockey team in 1912, but that was only the beginning of a number of links down the years. Fitz was commissioned into the A.S.C. on 16 Aug. 1905 and promoted Lieutenant on 16 Aug. 1907. At the outbreak of war he was promoted Captain and Temporary Major, and saw service in France and also Egypt. He was three times mentioned in despatches and was awarded the D.S.O. and M.C. After the War he pursued a distinguished career, culminating in his appointment as Inspector R.A.S.C. from 1940-43 with the rank of Major-General. E.S.H. was Assistant Inspector from 1940-42, based at the *War Office*, so would have worked closely with him. And their paths continued to cross after retirement. He appears with E.S.H. in the photo of retired officers taken in 1950 (*see page 105*), and in the following year partnered him in a golf foursome between retired officers and serving officers in July 1951. (*See Diary entry for Oct.23*)

Godley: Francis William Crewe Godley (*born 25 Jan. 1993*), was behind E.S.H. in his training but they overlapped at Aldershot. He has only one entry in the *Diary*—the rather cryptic note about dropping off his dog at Cheltenham. He was commissioned into the A.S.C. on 7 Feb. 1912, ending the War as an Acting Major and retiring from the Army in 1923. (*See Diary entry for Aug.5*)

Growse: Hugh Edward Growse (*born 3 Oct. 1883*) was a colleague of E.S.H. in the South Wales Borderers, having been commissioned into that regiment on 27 Sept. 1905 (There is a picture of Growse in E.S.H.'s 1909 photo book when they were together in India). Growse later transferred to the Indian Army and was promoted Captain on 27 Sept. 1914 around the time of his arrival in France with the 15th Sikhs. (*See Diary entry for Oct.22*)

Humphreys: Lionel George Humphreys (*spelt 'Humphries' in the Diary*) (*born 28 May 1991*) was at Aldershot at the same time as E.S.H., and played with him in the Corps hockey team in 1912. He was commissioned into the A.S.C. on 3 Sept. 1910. As noted in the *Diary*, he was taken prisoner on 2 Sept. 1914 along with Capt. Bell, but continued his career with the R.A.S.C. after the War and into World War II, reaching the rank of Brigadier. (*See Diary entry for Sept.3*)

Jenkins: Arthur de Brisay Jenkins (*born 2 Nov. 1891*) was on the same *Junior Officers' Course* as E.S.H., having been commissioned into the A.S.C. on 4 Dec. 1911. He was promoted Lieutenant on 4 Feb. 1914, Temporary Captain on 30 Nov. 1914, Captain on 4 Feb. 1917 and Acting Major on 27 Jul. 1921. During World War I he saw service in France and Belgium and then in 1917-18 in British, German and Portuguese East Africa, Nyasaland and Northern

Army Service Corps First Annual Tennis Tournament—Some of the Competitors

Back Row—J.L.G.Carter, H.A.C.Gardner, Capt. G.V.Hunt, C.V.Holbrook, G.E.Hodder, Capt. T.W.Hollins, H.A.Courtenay*, U.S.Holden, Capt. G.L.Peterson, **E.S.Hacker**, P.C.Goldney, Capt. A.M.Wilson, W.E.W.Howard, Capt. E.P.Blencowe.

Middle Row—F.E.M.Milner-Jones, Capt. G.N.Humphreys, A.G.Saulez*, Capt. J.A.D.Bell*, Capt. W.M.Parker, Bt-Maj. E.Gibb DSO, Capt. J.C.Browne, Capt. H.M.Caddell, Capt. F.W.Stringer, Capt. J.L.Jesse*

Front Row—Major H.C.Wilder*, Major P.M.Davies, Capt. A.Berger, Capt. H.A.Jones, Lieut-Col. W.G.R.Boyce DSO, Col. T.J. O'Dell CB CMG, Lieut-Col. R.Ford DSO, Major E.C.F.Gillespie, Bt-Maj. H.A.D.Richards, Capt. N.G.Anderson DSO.

* Mentioned in the Diary.

Rhodesia, and was mentioned in dispatches. From May to July 1919 he was in Russia with the British forces supporting the anti-Bolshevik cause in the North. After the War he continued with his career reaching the rank of Brigadier in World War II. (*See Diary entry for Sept.27*)

Jesse: John Leonard Jesse (*born 4 Apr. 1876*) was Adjutant of the Service Companies at Aldershot when E.S.H. was doing his part 2 of the *Junior Officers' Course*, and he also appears as one of the tennis players in the photo on page 95. He was commissioned into the Royal Marines on 1 Jan. 1897. He transferred to the A.S.C. on 3 Jan. 1900, and fought in the South African War. He was promoted Lieutenant on 3 Jan. 1901 and Captain on 7 Apr. 1902. During the World War I he saw service in Italy as well as France and Belgium and by 1919 had reached the rank of Temporary Colonel. In 1924 his rank as Colonel was made substantive and he was appointed Assistant Director of Supplies and Transport in Malta. In Jan. 1926 he went to the *War Office* as Assistant Director of Transport. He is recorded in the *Corps Journal* as playing against E.S.H. in the Handicap Doubles in the Corps Tennis Tournament in July 1921 and as being at the *Corps Club* 'At Home' and Dinner with him in June 1927. (*See Diary entry for Sept.23*)

McCaskill: Kenneth Douglas Fraser McCaskill (*born 17 Sept. 1989*) was a year ahead of E.S.H. in his training, but they overlapped at Aldershot. He was commissioned into the York and Lancaster Regiment on 6 Feb. 1909, and transferred to the A.S.C. on 1 Oct. 1910. During World War I he saw service in France and Belgium and from 1916 in the Balkans. At some point after the War he transferred to the Indian Army, and by 1936 was a Lieut-Colonel in the R.I.A.S.C. (*See Diary entries for Sept.6 & 26*)

Laird: Archibald Henry Montgomery Laird (*born 11 Aug. 1887*) was also a year ahead of E.S.H. in his training, but they overlapped at Aldershot. He was commissioned into the South Staffordshire Regiment on 19 Sept. 1908 and transferred to the A.S.C. on 1 Oct. 1910. A Lieutenant still in 1914, he was attached to H.Q., and promoted Captain and Brevet Major on October 30, not long after the diary entries for September 25 and 26. After the War he at some point joined the Royal Indian Army Service Corps and is listed in 1936 as Assistant Director of Supplies and Transport and Embarkation Commissioner for the Presidency and Assam District. (*See Diary entries for Sept.25 & 26*)

Martin: Charles Jasper Martin (*born on 2 Dec. 1888*) was a 2nd Lieutenant in the Connaught Rangers when he transferred to the A.S.C. on 4 Dec. 1912. His time at Aldershot overlapped with that of E.S.H., and the single entry in the *Diary* implies that they knew each other. He was in Gallipoli in Sept. and Oct. 1915. After the War in Dec. 1923 he was appointed Adjutant at Aldershot. He retired from the Army some time before 1929. (*See Diary entry for Aug.5*)

Morrison: Stanley Walter Morrison (*born 9 Mar. 1885*) has a lot of entries in the *Diary* and seems to have been generally helpful to E.S.H.. He was commissioned into the A.S.C. on 27 May 1908, promoted Lieutenant on 26 May 1911 and Captain and Temporary Major on 7 Oct. 1914. He continued in the R.A.S.C. after the War, reaching the rank of Major, and retiring sometime in the early 1930's. (*See Diary entries for Sept.26, Oct.15,18, Nov.4,12,18,21 & 26*)

Parkin: Herbert Denis Parkin (*born 31 Dec. 1886*) was commissioned into the Northamptonshire Regiment on 27 May 1908. He transferred to the A.S.C. on 2 Oct. 1911—the same date as E.S.H., He does not seem, however, to have been part of the same course as E.S.H., though still overlapping with him at Aldershot. After the War he saw service in Egypt and Shanghai amongst other places and reached the rank of Lieut-Colonel in the mid-1930's. (*See Diary entry for Sept.27*)

Purchas: Major E.G.Purchas was E.S.H.'s 'Skipper' in South Africa in 1911 with the South Wales Borderers (*see Diary entry for Nov.19*). An older man, he had been made Captain on 28 May 1898 and Brevet Major on 29 Nov. 1900. On 29 Nov. 1911 he was placed in the Reserve of Officers and listed as Major. As such he would be a likely candidate for a Railway Transport Officer. On the Western Front almost any station of importance had an R.T.O., whose job it was to 'facilitate' the transport of troop trains and assist soldiers rejoining their units from leave or hospital. (*See Diary entries for Nov.19 & 20*)

Reckitt: John Thorpe Reckitt (*born 13 Sept. 1890*) was a year ahead of E.S.H. in his training at Aldershot, but they overlapped. Commissioned into the A.S.C. on 23 Feb. 1910, he was promoted Lieutenant on 23 Feb. 1913. During World War I he served in France and Belgium and was awarded the M.C. In 1919 he was with the Expeditionary Force to Mesopotamia and Iraq as Deputy Assistant Director of Mechanical Transport. After the War he overlapped briefly with E.S.H. as an Instructor at the R.A.S.C. Training College in 1926. In World War II he reached the rank of Brigadier as Deputy Director of Supplies and Transport Northern Command. (*See Diary entry for Sept.26*)

Robinson: William Pasley Robinson was at Aldershot on the *Short M.T. Course* in Oct. 1911 when E.S.H. first arrived there. He had been commissioned into The Royal Munster Fusiliers on 28 Apr. 1902 and transferred to the A.S.C. on 1 Oct. 1902, and fought briefly in the South African War. He was promoted Captain on 1 Jan. 1911 and Major on 30 Oct. 1914. During World War I he saw service in France and Belgium, was three times mentioned in despatches and awarded the D.S.O. and O.B.E.. After the War he was Deputy Director of Transport and Adviser for M.T. Services in India until 1924, seeing service on the North West Frontier. He ended his career as a Colonel and retired in the early 1930's. (*See Diary entries for Aug.27,28 & Nov.23*)

Saulez: Alfred Gordon Saulez (*born 18 Dec. 1885*) joined the *Short M.T. Course* at Aldershot in October 1911 around the time that E.S.H. joined the *Junior Officers' Course*. He was also in the same hockey team as E.S.H. in 1912 and is pictured with him in the photo on page 95. He was commissioned into the A.S.C. on 3 Feb. 1906 and was promoted Captain and Temporary Major on 5 Aug. 1914. In 1920 he was serving in Mesopotamia. (*See Diary entries for Sept.6,8 & 16*)

Spafford: Percy Lionel Spafford (*born 9 Feb. 1890*) was with E.S.H. on the same *Junior Officers' Course* at Aldershot and also on the same *Long M.T. Course*. He was commissioned into the A.S.C. on 7 Dec. 1910 and promoted Lieutenant on 7 Dec. 1913. He was promoted Temporary Captain on 30 Nov. 1914 (the same date as E.S.H.), was three times mentioned in dispatches and was awarded the O.B.E. in July 1919. Much later in his career he was appointed a Chief Instructor at the *R.A.S.C. Training Centre* at Aldershot from 1934 to 1937, after which he was promoted Lieut-Colonel. (*See Diary entries for Sept.12 & 26, Oct.10, Nov.4 & 21*)

Swabey: William Spedding Swabey (*born 26 Feb. 1871*) was commissioned into the Yorkshire Light Infantry on 12 Mar. 1892. He transferred to the A.S.C. on 1 Apr. 1894, was promoted Captain on 25 Aug. 1898 and Major on 1 Aug. 1905. What his connection with E.S.H. was is not clear, though the tone of the *Diary* entry rather implies that he knew him fairly well. The entry also refers to his recent promotion to Lieut-Colonel on 15 Oct. 1914. (*See Diary entry for Nov.23*)

Smith: Robert Hunter Smith (*born 25 Oct. 1892*) was another that E.S.H. overlapped with at Aldershot, having been commissioned into the A.S.C. on 7 Feb. 1912. During World War I he served in France and Belgium until Jan. 1915 and was Deputy Assistant Quartermaster General Home Forces from Dec. 1916 until May 1918. He was then sent to Russia, returning in Oct. 1919. He was appointed O.C. Gentlemen Cadets at the *Royal Military College* in Aug. 1929, and was in Egypt as Deputy Assistant Director of Supplies and Transport from 1931-34. He was made Brevet Lieut-Colonel in 1934. (*See Diary entry for Nov.18*)

Warren: William Robert Vaughan Warren (*born 28 Feb. 1889*) was commissioned into the Royal Artillery on 9 May 1909. He transferred to the A.S.C. on 2 Oct. 1911—the same date as E.S.H., and they were together on the same *Junior Officers' Course* and *Long M.T. Course* at Aldershot. Like E.S.H. he was promoted Lieutenant on 2 Oct. 1912 and Temporary Captain on 30 Nov. 1914. During World War I he was twice mentioned in dispatches and was awarded the O.B.E. and M.C.. Later in his career he saw service in Egypt in 1936 and was promoted Lieut-Colonel on 15 Aug. 1937. He is in the 1950 photo of retired officers on page 105. (*See Diary entries for Aug.27 & Sept.24*)

Wilder: Harry Carleton Wilder (*born 1 Mar. 1870*) was in Aldershot when E.S.H. was doing his training there and appears in the photo on page 95. He was commissioned into the Leicestershire Regiment on 15 Mar. 1893. Later he transferred to the A.S.C. and was promoted Captain on 14 Jun. 1900 and Major on 15 Oct. 1909. He was appointed Deputy Assistant Director of Transport on 11 Oct. 1914 and it was in this capacity that E.S.H. had dealings with him at H.Q. He finished the War as O.C. R.A.S.C. Gibralter, having been promoted Lieut-Colonel on 24 Feb. 1915, and retired from the Army in 1920. (*See Diary entries for Oct.20, Nov.18 & 25*)

Appendix 4
Extracts from the Corps Journal
(*Reproduced by permission of the Royal Logistic Corps Museum*)

Names with a star against them are mentioned in the Diary

15 October 1911

The undermentioned officers joined at Aldershot on 2nd October on probation as Second Lieutenants—

    Lieut.   E.S.C.Grone, West African Regt.
    "   H.D.Parkin*, Northampton Regt.
    "   K.E.Partridge, Dorset Regt.
    "   P.J.Whitty, Royal Irish Regt.
    "   B.N.Dalton, Bedford Regt.
    "   R.A.Thompson, Northampton Regt.
    "   **E.S.Hacker**, South Wales Borderers.
    2nd Lieut. W.R.V.Warren*, Royal Artillery.
    "   E.C.Pinder*, Dorset Regt.
    Lieut.   B.O.Smyth, Northampton Regt.
    2nd Lieut. A.J.Clifton, Durham L.I.
    "   L.W.Purchas, Leicester Regt.
    "   J.Angell, Royal Irish Fusiliers.

15 January 1912

The following officers proceeded from Aldershot to the stations named on 8th January—
    2nd Lieuts J.Armstrong, R.H.Growse, **E.S.Hacker**, and E.C.Pinder* have been posted to Service Companies, Aldershot.

15 February 1912

Hockey—3rd round of the Army Hockey Tournament.
Team—Goal, Dvr. Collier; backs, Corpl. Maloney and Lieut. Godfray; half-backs, Lieuts Humphreys*, Archibald* and Fitzherbert*; forwards, Lieuts **Hacker**, Allden*, Saulez* and Tudor.

15 August 1912

This number contains details for the Army Service Corps First Annual Tennis Tournament in which E.S.H. took part, together with a photo (reproduced on page 95).

Handicap Singles 1st round
    Jones owe 15 beat **Hacker** rec. 15 6-4 6-1

Handicap Doubles 1st round

Milner-Jones and **Hacker** rec. 3/6 beat Wilder* and Lt-Col. Wilson rec. 3/6 6-9 7-5

2nd round
Milner-Jones and **Hacker** beat Courtenay* and Thompson 6-3 6-4

Semi-Final
Lt-Col. Boyce and Anderson beat Milner-Jones and **Hacker**

18 January 1913

The following officers have been ordered from commands to the Training Establishment for further instruction (3rd stage Junior Officers' Course)—

    Lieut. W.R.V.Warren* from Bulford
    2nd Lieut. P.L.Spafford*   "
       "   G.A.Beale-Browne, from Bulford
       "   N.R. de la L. Gill, from Portsmouth
       "   W.E.W.Howard, from Devonport
       "   A.D.Butterworth, from Dublin
       "   A. de B. Jenkins*, from Dublin
       "   H.T.Mellish, from Curragh
       "   C.W.R.Langmaid, from Curragh
       "   E.W.F.Aylwin-Foster, from Curragh
    Lieut. J.C.Armstrong, from Service Companies
       "   **E.S.Hacker**,   "   "   "
       "   E.C.Pinder*   "   "   "
    2nd Lieut. R.H.Growse, "   "   "
    Lieut. M.N.Dalton, from York
    2nd Lieut. R.H.Verney, now with 52 Coy
       "   M.J.H.Bruce, "   "

August 1913

The following moves have been ordered (*Amongst other names*)—
    Lieut. **E.S.Hacker**, Aldershot to Curragh
      "   E.C.Pinder*, Aldershot to Cork
    2nd-Lieut. P.L.Spafford*, Aldershot to Devonport
      "   A. de B. Jenkins*, Aldershot to Cork

October 1913

The following officers have been selected to attend the long course in mechanical transport duties, at Aldershot, commencing of 1st November 1913—
    Major H.J.Russell
    Capt. H.D.Russell, D.S.O.
    Lieut. W.R.V.Warren*
      "   W.E.W.Howard
      "   J.C.Armstrong

        Lieut. **E.S.Hacker**
          "   E.C.Pinder*
        2nd-Lieut. E.W.F.Aylwin-Foster
          "   P.L.Spafford*
          "   G.E.Beale-Browne

July 1921

Royal Army Service Corps Club—*Amongst those listed as being present at the At Home and Dinner held at the Hyde Park Hotel, London, on 3rd June, 1921, are the following, who are mentioned in the Diary—*
    Colonel W.S.Swabey*, CB, CMG, CBE
    Major E.H.Fitzherbert*, DSO, MC
    Captain **E.S.Hacker**, MC
    Captain E.B.Rowcroft*
    Captain P.L.Spafford*, OBE

August 1921

Lawn Tennis Tournament 1921: Handicap Doubles—In the first round a good match was played between Colonel J.M.Young and Lt-Colonel J.L.Jesse* against Capt. Rountree and Capt. **Hacker**, the latter winning with the games at 4-6, 7-5, 6-3. In the second round Capt. Rountree and Capt. **Hacker** had another hard match against Capt. W.C.Price and Lieut. O'Neill, being beaten at 9-7, 6-8, 6-1.

June 1927

R.A.S.C. Golfing Society—The Annual Meeting was held on the West Surrey Course, Entor Green, near Godalming, on April 28th and 29th, under perfect conditions, which was a welcome change after last year's experience in the weather.
    Capt. **Hacker** is listed as playing in the Command Foursomes Championship and the Command Foursomes Handicap, partnered by Major Arden (a lifelong friend, known as 'P.A.' and well remembered by the Editor). Major L.C..Bearne* and Major G.K.Archibald* appear in the same list.

July 1927

Royal Army Service Corps Club—*Amongst those listed as being present at the Annual 'At-home' and Dinner, which took place at the Hotel Victoria (Edward VII Rooms), Northumberland Avenue, London, on Tuesday, 21st June, are the following who are mentioned in the Diary—*
    Major G.K.Archibald*
    Major L.C.Bearne*
    Major E.H.Fitzherbert*
    Major H.D.Parkin*
    Major J.T.Reckitt*
    Major R.H.Smith*
    Captain W.H.Clarke*
    Captain E.S.Hacker
    Captain L.G.Humphreys*

February 1931

Bulford: Christmas—The next function was the Sergeants' Mess Children's Christmas Tree, which was held on the 22nd instant, and was attended by about 200 members and their children. The C.O. and officers present at the station also attended, and **Mrs Hacker**, ably assisted by Father Christmas, concluded a most happy afternoon by presenting each child with some toy or suitable present.

On the 23rd the All Ranks' Christmas Tree was held, and was voted by all to be a huge success. The P.R.I. (Major **E.S.Hacker**) and his band of willing helpers succeeded in organizing this event with the utmost success, and close on 400 sat down to tea in the Garrison Institute. The tea was followed by a cinema show, and then Father Christmas again appeared, and assisted Mrs Inglefield to present each child with a suitable present. The gathering included the whole of the R.A.S.C. establishment, military and civilian, who are serving on the Plain, including Tidworth, Larkhill, Salisbury, etc.

May 1931

The R.A.S.C. Bona-fide Military Meeting, 1931—This was the first occasion that the Annual Corps Meeting has been run under National Hunt rules. . . The meeting was held on March 14th on the new course at Windmill Hill, near Tidworth. . . The new course at Windmill Hill is an excellent one, both for spectators and riders. The fences are plain and straightforward, there being but one small open ditch and no water. All those who rode pronounced themselves well pleased.

Second Race—R.A.S.C. Lightweight Race
    Also ran: Major **Hacker's** Martha IV (Capt. Daubeny)
Fourth Race—R.A.S.C. Heavyweight Race
    Also ran: Major **Hacker's** Lorna Doone VII (Capt. Burlton)

This was a disappointing race, though it gave the crowd plenty of thrills. Lorna Doone VII led over the first two fences, but Kingsley refused at the second fence, and in doing so cannoned heavily into Cheerilass, whose rider was temporarily knocked out. . . In the meantime Lorna Doone VII was now half a mile ahead, and the race looked all over 'bar the shouting'. However, after completing the first circuit, the mare was noticed to be fencing poorly and she was obviously tiring, whilst Kingsley was now galloping well and was quickly reducing the gap, with Countess over a hundred yards behind. Four fences from home Kingsley passed Lorna Doone VII, now reduced almost to a walk.

However the race was not yet over! At the next fence (the open ditch) Kingsley again refused and threw his rider into the ditch. Major Arden, however, scrambled out quickly, and at his next attempt got Kingsley over the fence, followed by Lorna Doone VII, which only just scrambled through, with Countes on her heels. At the penultimate fence, Lorna Doone VII, which was now quite done, turned a complete somersault! Countess was unable to overhaul Kingsely, which won by almost a distance.

December 1931

Bulford—The opening meet of the Harriers took place at the Royal Artillery Mess on October 20th. The weather was dull with a cold wind. A slight drizzle started as we moved off shortly after 2 p.m., but cleared up later. The cold wind and the dry state of the ground offered poor prospects for a good hunt . . . Unfortunately, for various reasons, very few of the Corps were able to turn out, the only followers being **Mrs Hacker**, Mrs Seymour and Capt. Geddes.

November 1932

The Corps Golfing Society held their Annual Meeting at Woking on Tuesday, September 27th—

Handicap 11 and over: Major **E.S.Hacker** (handicap 17) - 2 up.

The Southern Command Golf Championships are playing shortly. In the Singles, scratch and handicap, the Corps was represented by Majors W.R.Warren*, **E.S.Hacker** and P.A.Arden, and Capt. R.K.Holmes. Major **Hacker** returned a net score of 143 against a bogey score of 148 in the Handicap event, but this was not good enough.

January 1933

Golf—On November 14th, Major **Hacker** collected as many golfers as he could find to take down to Broadstone, with the idea of giving a good beating to our brethren of the Aldershot Command. He felt that our peregrinations to the courses out and around Aldershot should cease, and that it was the duty of golfers at Aldershot to pay us a visit and enjoy the bracing air of the Southern Command.

The idea was a great success, and Major **Hacker** collected golfers from as far away as Devonport, Tidworth, Larkhill, Salisbury and Bovington, who met punctually at Broadstone at 10 a.m.

The Aldershot contingent, many of whom had spent the previous evening at Bournemouth, arrived shortly afterwards, and as we were blessed with a perfect November morning, without a breath of wind, everyone enjoyed an excellent day's golf.

Singles were played in the morning and foursomes in the afternoon, and the net result of the whole day's play was a win by three holes to Major **Hacker's** team—a remarkably close finish.

We are greatly indebted to the members of the Broadstone Club for their courtesy and kindness to us, and we heartily congratulate Major **Hacker** on the success of the day and hope that, encouraged by this success he will arrange further fixtures.

September 1934

The Regimental Coach—The team and coach were sent to Salisbury by train on Tuesday, 5th June, for the Royal Counties Show. We competed in the ring on Friday, 8th June, against seven other teams, but only managed to gain 'Reserve' to the R.E. team.

The Marathon was run the following afternoon, and we carried a strong contingent of passengers from the Southern Command, amongst whom were Mrs Pereira, **Major and Mrs Hacker**, and Capt. and Mrs R.K.Holmes. Here again we failed to please the judge, who awarded the prize to the R.E. team.

September 1935

The Union Jill Club—On 28th June there was a special meeting held in the Annexe, and **Mrs Hacker** introduced our new President, Mrs Beuttler. There was a record attendance, and Mrs Beuttler received a warm welcome. Mrs Green won one competition, and 'A' Team won the Relay Race.

December 1936

Chatham—By the time these notes go to press our Commanding Officer, Lieut-Col. **E.S.Hacker**, MC, will have sailed for overseas in s.s.*Narkunda*; our loss is Gibraltar's gain. All ranks respectfully wish Col. and Mrs **Hacker** all the best for the future in their new station and will always remember with great pleasure his far-too-short tenure of command at Chatham, where his encouragement and personality were much appreciated.

October 1937

Gibraltar—*Royal Gibraltar Yacht Club Cup*—Won by *Lassie* (sailed by Lieut-Col. **Hacker** and Capt. Warren, R.M.).

January 1938

Gibraltar—The final results of the yachting season showed that *Missing Link* (Brigadier Currey and Capt. Bond) was the second most successful yacht in 'B' Class, and *Lassie* (Lieut-Col. **Hacker** with Capt. Warren, R.M., or Lieut-Col. Brinton) was third.

May 1939

Gibraltar—Shooting is still proving very popular, and the spice of this month's entertainment was the shoot for the Hacker Cup, very kindly presented by Lieut-Col. **Hacker**. Teams comprised of officers and W.Os, Staff-Sergeants and Sergeants, Butchers and Bakers, Clerks and M.T. Section took part, and the Staff-Sergeants and Sergeants finished with a narrow margin over the M.T. Section. Lieut-Col. **Hacker** presented the cup and miniatures to the winning team . . . and congratulated the team on their success. S/Sergt. Hyde replied with a few well-chosen words, and we repaired to the Sergeants' Mess, where the cup was duly filled—and emptied.

We would like to thank our Colonel for this presentation, which was made when we formed our Rifle Club, and we hope that this year's musketry results will justify the interest he has taken in the Club.

August 1939

Gibraltar—**Mrs Hacker**, wife of our C.O., gave a very pleasant garden party for the wives and children of the Company, which was thoroughly enjoyed by all who attended.`

It is with the greatest regret that we have to say good-bye to our C.O., who sailed for the United Kingdom on 25th June to take up the appointment of C.I.S.T. We wish him and Mrs Hacker a very pleasant journey and the best of luck for the future.

Lieut-Col. **Hacker** has been the starter for the Gibraltar Jockey Club for the past two seasons. He was Chairman of the Gibraltar Museum and Hon. Secretary of the Soldiers', Sailors' and Airmen's Families' Association, whilst **Mrs Hacker** has been Hon. Secretary of the Girl Guides Association, Gibraltar Branch, and has served on the Committees of Brympton School, the Arts and Crafts Society, the S.S. & A.F.A., and the Mothers' Union (Army Branch).

Corps Journal for August 1950

This photograph, from outside Butler Officers' Mess, shows some of the very many personalities who were present during the 'At Home'
Front—Maj-Gen. H.M.Whitty; Lt-Col. G.Blount-Dinwiddie; Brig. J.K.Gillespie; Brig. W.N.White; Maj-Gen. E.H.Fitzherbert*; Brig. H.C.Goodfellow.
First Row—Maj-Gen. T.W.Richardson; Maj-Gen. Sir R.Kerr; Maj-Gen. F.S.Clover; Col. J.H.Morris; Maj-Gen. M.S.Brander; Col. A.C.Robinson; Brig. A.G.W.Bevin; Maj-Gen. C.M.Smith; Lt-Col. W.R.V.Warren*.
Second Row—Brig. R.M.Airey; Brig. C.E.R.Ince**; Col. N.F.Penruddock**; Lt-Col. A.B.Wakelin; Maj. F.H.Barbor; Col. H.G.C.Hawkins; **Brig. E.S.Hacker**; Maj-Gen. J.E.Witt.
Third Row—Lt-Col. F.H.Freeman-Cowen; Col. J.A.Middleton; Brig. W.H.D.Ritchie; Brig. J.C.Armstrong.
Back—Lt-Col. T.C.King; Col. I.K.Price; Col. A.S.Parkin.

* *Mentioned in the Diary* ** *Known personally to the Editor (some others were familiar names)*

January 1944

Retirement: Brigadier **E.S.Hacker**, M.C., A.M.I.Mech.E—Brigadier **Hacker** attained the age of retirement on 10th October, 1942, and was retained on the active list supernumerary to establishment. He was placed on retired pay on 30th November 1943, with the honorary rank of Brigadier, and is re-employed.

He was born on 10th November 1887, and was first commissioned in the Militia, serving with the Duke of Edinburgh's Royal Garrison Artillery. He was granted a Regular commission in the South Wales Borderers on 27th May 1908, and transferred to the A.S.C. on 2nd October 1911.

He was one of the small but distinguished band of A.S.C. officers who before the last war foresaw the vast potentialities of M.T., and by their zeal and vision established a very high standard of mechanical efficiency in the Corps.

In the First World War he served in France and Belgium from 15th August to the end of 1914, and again from May 1916* until the Armistice. For his services he was mentioned in despatches and was awarded the M.C. He was promoted Captain in September 1915.

For some months in 1920 he held the appointment of D.A.D. of Transport (Class B) in France, and then returned for three years to regimental duty. From 1923 to 1927 he was an instructor under the Chief Inspector of Mechanical Transport at Aldershot. In 1932 he was appointed D.A.D.S.T. Southern Command, and on relinquishing this appointment four years later, was selected to command the R.A.S.C. in Gibraltar.

He was promoted Lieutenant-Colonel on 2nd March 1936, and Colonel on 2nd March 1939. In the summer of the latter year he was appointed Chief Inspector of Supplementary Transport and carried through the purchase of impressed and 'B' vehicles for the Expeditionary Force.

That very onerous task completed, he was appointed Chief Inspector of Mechanical Transport in February 1940. On 15th May of the same year, during the most critical phase of the Battle of France, he was selected for the appointment of Assistant Inspector R.A.S.C., which carried with it the rank of Brigadier. He held this very important post for the next two and a half years.

It was a period of great and rapid expansion in all branches of the Corps. Fresh commitments arose almost daily in every overseas theatre of the war; new units had to be formed, trained, mobilized and sent abroad. The efficiency and outstanding achievements of R.A.S.C. units in all theatres are a tribute to the Assistant Inspector's pioneering work.

In September 1942 Brigadier **Hacker** went to South-Eastern Command as D.D.S.T., and held this appointment until his retirement two months ago.

Brigadier **Hacker** was a very keen supporter of the point-to-point. His mare, 'Lorna Doone', won the Heavy-weight Cup in 1928 and 1930, and his two entries won the Heavy-weight Team Cup for Aldershot in 1928 and for Bulford in 1929.

This error (1916 instead of 1915) seems to have originated from an error in the Army Lists

September 1951

Golf: Retired Officers v. Serving Officers—This match, inaugurated last year, took place on the West Hill golf Course, on Monday 16th July and was a decisive win for the Retired Officers by 12½ matches to 6½.

Singles—Brig. **E.S.Hacker** 0 v. Major Thompson (3 & 2) 1.
Foursomes—Fitzherbert* and **Hacker** (5 & 4) 1 v. Whitty and Thompson 0.

*Major Thompson about to drive, watched by Brigadier **Hacker***

Appendix 5
'Old Bill'

Old Bill was E.S.H.'s smooth-haired fox terrier, who was his companion for a large part of his time in France. He was named after the famous character in Bruce Bairnsfather's cartoons, the pipe-smoking veteran with the walrus moustache, who is best remembered for his comment from the bottom of a shell hole in which he was taking shelter: 'Well, If you know of a better 'ole go to it!'

E.S.H. and Bruce Bairnsfather were contemporaries at Trinity College, Stratford-upon-Avon, and are said to have shared a study. Following his time there, instead of making the Army his career, Bruce Bairnsfather studied art in London, but joined the Royal Warwickshire Regiment on the outbreak of war. He sent comic drawings from the Front to the *Bystander* and these proved so successful that he was made Officer-Cartoonist and transferred to the *Intelligence Department* of the *War Office*, where they hoped he could be used for propaganda purposes. E.S.H. didn't have a very high opinion of his artistic ability and was once heard to remark: 'He couldn't draw for toffees—only Old Bill and shell holes'.

E.S.H. makes no mention of any dog belonging to him in the Diary, but a press cutting from the *Daily Mirror*, probably dated 1921, has this caption underneath Old Bill's photo: '*Old Bill, the famous terrier who went to France with the R.A.S.C. in 1914 and was the last to leave, will be remembered by thousands of soldiers*'. E.S.H. had had a smooth-haired fox terrier before, when he was in India (the Editor has some photos of Gyp), and there were others after the War. Whether Old Bill went with him to France in 1914, or was 'adopted' by him later is not clear, but they were together for a large part of the War. At all events he became quite famous and was treated as a mascot by the A.S.C. troops. E.S.H. had to leave him behind with a brother officer, when he returned to England in 1920, and was not very pleased when the latter exploited him for publicity purposes. E.S.H. remembered Old Bill with great affection, and had a photo of him on his desk for many years.

Appendix 6
E.S.H.'s Army Records Relevant Entries

| ROYAL ARMY SERVICE CORPS | HACKER |
| Edward Sidney | E.S.H. |

1. *Where Educated: Schools*: Newton College,
   Trinity College Stratford-on-Avon
   Date of Birth: 10th November 1887
   Place of Birth: Newton Abbot
   Religious Denomination: C. of E.
   Nationality of Officer: British
   Father: British
   Mother: British

2. *Name and Address of Next-of-kin*:
   Mr George L. Hacker, Dormer Venn, Westcott, Nr Dorking, Surrey.
   Name and Address of Bankers or Agents.
   Messrs Holt & Co., 3 Whitehall Place, London S.W.

3. *If Married, Name of Wife*: Carla Lanyon.
   Date of Marriage: 30. 7. 27
   Names of Children Living:

George Lanyon	27. 12. 28	Male
Carlotta Leila	6. 4. 31	Female
Edward Arthur	1. 6. 32	Male

4. Schools and Courses of Instruction

School of Instruction	Aldershot	1911	Passed
Long M.T. Course	Aldershot	1913	Passed
Works Course Messrs Thorneycroft	Basingstoke	1920-22	
No 8 War Course (Summer)	Aldershot	1931	Qualified Authority: 43/RASC/916
No 9 War Course (Winter)	Aldershot	20.10.31 17.11.31	Qualified Authority: 43/RASC/914
48th Course Senior Officers' School	Sheerness	30.9-18.12 1935	Completed Authority: AO 12/1936

6. *Examination for Promotion*

    Lieutenant   1910
    Captain   1924 *Special Certificate*: (C)
                       1925 *Special certificate*: (d) (g)

7. *(a) Foreign Languages*: Lower Urdu, Higher Urdu, Lower Baluchi
   (b) Knowledge of Foreign Countiries: India, South Africa, France
   (e) Professional Qualifications: A.M.I.Mech.E.

8. *Campaigns*:

    The Great War   France: 18.8.14 to 5.12.14
                                France: 18.5.15 to 18.10.20

9. *Honours and Rewards, including Mentions in Despatches*:

    Mentioned in Despatches   *L.G. 15.6.16*
    M.C.   *L.G. 1.1.17*
    Coronation Medal 1937

Extra-Regimental Employment:

D.A.D.T. (Cl.B.B.)	9.3.20 to 31.7.20	*L.G.17.5.20 & 20.12.20*
D.A.D.S.T. Southern Cd.	21.1.32 to 20.1.36	*L.G.20.12.20 & 28.1.36*
C.I.S.T.	1.7.39	*L.G.11.7.39*

10. *Record of Movements*:

Under Instruction	Aldershot	2.10.11
Duty	Curragh	8.7.13
Long M.T.Course	Aldershot	1.11.13
Duty	Bulford	1.8.14
Expeditionary Force 5th Cav. Bde Ammn Park	France	18.8.14
Duty	Home	6.12.14
Expeditionary Force 14th Supply Column	Framce	10.5.15
O.C. 'R' Corps Supply Column	France	3.2.17
O.C. Hdqrs 'R' Corps M.T.Column	France	10.3.18
No.7 M.T. V.R.P. No.3 District.	France	12.2.19
D.A.D.T. Forward District	France	9.3.20
Headquarters British Troops France & Flanders	France	-
O.C. R.A.S.C. Forward Districts	France	4.8.20
	Home	18.10.20
M.T. Course at Thorneycroft Works	Basingstoke	1.11.20
On strength of 1050 M.T.Coy (re-designated 'P' M.T.Coy)		
Emergency Duty in connection with strike	M.T.D.Bulford	12.4.21
Rejoined for Works Course at Thornycroft Works	Basingstoke	24.6.21

Record of Movements—continued

O.C. No.12 M.T. Company	Woolwich	14.11.22
'P' M.T. Company	Aldershot	30.?.23
35 M.T. Coy R.A.S.C.	Aldershot	7.7.27
O.C. 9 M.T. Coy	Aldershot	12.10.27
O.C. 36 M.T. Coy R.A.S.C.	Bulford	22.3.28
2nd in Command	Bulford	
D.A.D.S.T. Southern Command	Salisbury	21.1.32
		L.G. 26.1.32
Relinquished appt. of D.A.D.S.T. Southern Command	Salisbury	21.1.36
		L.G. 28.1.36
O.C. R.A.S.C.	Chatham	22.1.36
Embarked for	Gibraltar	13.11.36
Disembarked	Gibraltar	17.11.36
O.C. R.A.S.C.	Gibraltar	25.12.36
Leave UK 15.5.37 to 26.5.37	Gibraltar	
Leave UK 9.1.38 to 25.1.38	Gibraltar	
Leave UK 15.9.38 to 27.9.38	Gibraltar	
Embarked for UK	Gibraltar	25.6.39
Disembarked UK	Home	30.6.39
To be Chief Inspector Supplementary Transport	London	L.G. 11.7.39
Promoted Colonel with seniority 2.3.1939	London	L.G. 11.7.39
Relinquished appt Chief Inspector MT	London	15.5.40

Authority cs 261 S/4164

Appointed Asst. Inspector RASC and granted paid War Office   15.5.40
    duty rank Brigadier   Authority cs 261 S/4164
To be temporarily employed and granted unpaid duty rank   15.5.40
    of Brigadier and paid duty rank of Brigadier   Authority wo.0.54/40
Having attained age for retirement, is retained on   10.10.42
    active list sup. to Est.   L.G. 22.12.42
To relinquish D.D.S.T. H.Q.   (*Telep. 3/9/43 MS 1/1/2078*)   7.9.43
Relinquishes appt. as DDST & T/Brigadier (*1/2078/ dd 3/9/43*) 7.9.43
    Authority All/18/HQ/SFC/

To report immed. to H.Q. Aldershot Dist. as O.C. R.A.S.C.
    Rank of Lt/Col. on recall to Active List   10.12.43
    B.M. 1095 (AG80) D271 DD 88.12.43 Authority Pt1/4/43/HQ Ald Dist
Posted to O.C. R.A.S.C. Aldershot & Hants District   15.12.44
    Pt 2/2/HQ A & H   Authority Pt2/25/HQ Ald. Dist.
(*BM 1358/D491 d. 118.12.44*) Posted to H5 1Jtg Bn wap T.O.S.   15.12,44
    Authority Pt2/101/11TB
Ceased to be employed & granted Hon. rank of Brig.   26.2.45
    WOCC1 19/1/45   Authority L.G. sup B27/2/45

Promotion

South Wales Borderers

2/Lt.	27.5.08	

R.A.S.C.

On Probation for t'fer to A.S.C.	2.10.11	*L.G. 19.1.12*
		100/A.S.C./504
Finally transferred to A.S.C.	2.10.11	*L.G. 18.10.12*
2/Lt.	2.10.11	*L.G. 19.1.12*
Lieut.	2.10.12	*L.G. 18.10.12*
T/Capt.	30.11.14 to 14.9.15	*L.G. 13.1.15*
Capt.	13.9.15	*L.G. 26.1.16*
T/Maj.	15.9.15 to 19.1.21	*L.G. 2.5.16*
		& 18.1.21
Maj.	5.1.29	*L.G. 4.1.29*
Lt. Col.	2.3.36	*L.G. 10.3.36*
Colonel (with seniority 2.3.39)	1.7.39	*L.G. 11.7.39*
T/Brigadier	15.11.40	*W.O.O. 6/41*
Relinq. T/Brig.	7.9.43	*W.O.O. 39/43*
Lt. Col. own request	10.12.43	*L.G. 27.2.45/1*
Restored Colonel	26.2.45	*L.G. 27.2.45/2*

Appendix 7
Resources

Resources

There is an enormous amount of material available for anyone who wants to do research into the First World War, as the Editor quickly discovered when he began editing the Diary in 2006. More recently the Centenary Year has resulted in a fresh upsurge of books and other resources, many of them directly concerned with the period covered by the Diary. Here is a list of resource material which the Editor found particularly helpful.

General Books on World War I

The Great War: Based on the classic TV series, Corelli Barnett (BBC Worldwide Ltd, 2003).
A Military Atlas of the First World War, Arthur Banks (Leo Cooper, 1989).
The World War I Databook, John Ellis & Michael Cox (Aurum Press, 2001)
Roll of Honour, The Marquis de Ruvigny (Naval & Military Press).
List of Officers Taken Prisoner in the Various Theatres of War between August 1914 and November 1918 (Cox & Co.).
The Long Shadow: The Great War and the Twentieth Century, David Reynolds (Simon & Schuster UK Ltd, 2013). The Author seeks to balance the impression created of the War as a futile bloodbath in the mud of Flanders, by focussing on the big themes and so attempting to assess the true impact of 1914-18 on the 20th century.
Ring of Steel: Germany and Austria-Hungary at War, 1914-1918, Alexander Watson (Penguin 2014). In this book the major events of the war are seen from the perspective of Berlin and Vienna. Fundamentally a history of ordinary people and what they suffered. It is particularly important as providing a balance to the many accounts of the war from the Allies' point of view.
Meeting the Enemy: The Human Face of the Great War, Richard van Emden (Bloomsbury Paperbacks, 2014). A record of how contact was maintained between the two sides at many levels, which gives a new perspective on the lives of ordinary men and women caught up in extraordinary events.
The Long Trail: Soldiers' songs & slang 1914-18, John Brophy & Eric Partridge (Sphere Books Ltd, 1969).

Books on the Period Covered by the Diary

Catastrophe: Europe goes to War 1914, Max Hastings (William Collins 2014). The Author argues against the 'poets' view that the war was not worth winning, but was vital to the freedom of Europe, and his blend of top-down and bottom-up accounts brings alive those early weeks, which have so often been overlaid by the images of mud, wire and trenches. A 'must' for any serious researcher.

Invasion 1914: The Schlieffen Plan to the Battle of the Marne, Ian Senior (Osprey Publishing 2014). Accounts for English readers of the opening weeks of the First World War have been largely dominated by the B.E.F. although initially it only fielded 4 divisions, while the French and Germans provided 60 each. In this important book the Author seeks to redress the balance by describing the campaign from the French and German viewpoints.

The Old Contemptibles: The British Expeditionary Force, 1914, Robin Neillands (John Murray, 2004). A history specifically of the B.E.F. from its conception at the end of the 19th century to its demise in the water-logged trenches around Ypres. Note especially the first four chapters on the B.E.F. before 1914.

The Old Contmptibles: A Photographic History of the British Expeditionary Force August-December 1914, Keith Simpson (George Allen & Unwin, 1981).

1914: The Days of Hope, Lyn Macdonald (Penguin Books Ltd, 1989). Particularly valueable for the mass of original accounts the Author has collected.

Mons: The Retreat to Victory, John Terraine (B.T.Batsford Ltd, 1960). A detailed and authoritative account of the campaign.

Liaison 1914: A Narrative of the Great Retreat, Major-General Sir Edward Spears (Eyre & Spottiswoode, 1968). The Author was a young lieutenant in 1914, and as liaison officer with the French 5th Army, played a key part in the retreat. He was also in a unique position to observe events as they unfolded.

August 1914, Barbara Tuchman (Constable, 1962).

The Advance from Mons, 1914, Walter Bloem, translated from the German by G.C.Wynne (Peter Davies Ltd, 1930). The Author was a well-known German novelist, who served as a reserve captain in the 12th Brandenburg Grenadiers in 3 Corps of von Kluck's Army. Originally published in German in 1916, it gives unique insights into the events of 1914 from the German point of view.

From Mons to Loos, Major H.A.Stewart (Wm. Blackwood, 1917).

The Diary of a World War I Cavalry Officer, Brigadier-General Sir Archibald Home.

History of the Great War Based on Official Documents: France and Belgium, 1914, Brigadier-General J.E.Edmonds (The Imperial War Museum & The Battery Press Inc., 1996).

Books on Transport and the Army Service Corps

Military Transport of World War I, Chris Ellis (Blandford Press, 1970). Includes vintage and post war models, and vehicles from European countries and the U.S.A.

The World Encyclopedia of Trucks, Peter J. Davies (Hermes House, 2002).

The Handbook of Classic British Bikes (Abbeydale Press, 1999).

The Army Service Corps 1902-1918, Michael Young (Pen & Sword Books, 2000). A second edition (published in 2012 by Partizan Press) is now available with a greatly enlarged photographic section. Both editions are very full and detailed, with comprehensive annexes, and are ideal for the serious researcher.

The Royal Army Service Corps: A History of Transport and Supply in the British Army, Vol. 1, John Fortescue, Vol. 2, Colonel H.R.Beadon (The Naval and Military Press Ltd). Between them these two volumes cover the many campaigns by the British Army from William III's in Ireland in 1689 through to the North Russian Expedition in 1919. Very detailed and comprehensive.

The Turn of the Wheel: The History of the RASC 1919-1939, Major-General Patrick G. Turpin (Barracuda Books Ltd, 1988).

The Story of the Royal Army Service Corps 1939-1945, Published under the direction of the Institution of the R.A.S.C. (G.Bell & Sons Ltd, 1955).

The Story of the Royal Army Service Corps and the Royal Corps of Transport 1945-1982, Brigadier D.J.Sutton Editor in Chief (Leo Cooper 1983). This and the previous two books amount to official histories, and cover the whole period in great detail.

Waggoner's Way: The Royal Corps of Transport 1891-1991, Michael Young Editor (Baron 1993). Not so much a history of the R.C.T. and its predecessors, as a collection from journals of the Corps and photographs from the archives. Michael Young is a former Curator of the Royal Corps of Transport Museum.

History of the Great War based on Official Documents: Transportation on the Western Front 1914-1918, Colonel A.M.Henniker (The Imperial War Museum & Battery Press Inc, 1992). This volume is mainly about rail transport.

Other Resources

The website: www.1914-1918.net—'The Long Long Trail: The British Army in the Great War'. A comprehensive, detailed and most valuable resource.

The website: www.nationalarchives.gov.uk—the National Archives. For the medal roll and general information about army records.

The website: www.cwgc.org—Commonwealth War Graves Commission.

The Royal Logistic Corps Museum, Princess Royal Barracks, Deepcut, Camberley, GU16 6RW. For archival material including copies of the Corps Journal.

Army Personnel Centre, HQ Secretariat Historical Disclosures, Mail Point 400, Kentigern House, 65 Brown Street, Glasgow, G2 8EX For army records.

The Library of Birmingham (formerly The Birmingham Central Library). For a comprehensive military history section with access to Army Lists and other reference material.

The Public Record Office, Ruskin Avenue, Kew, Richmond, Surrey, TW9 4DU.

Printed in Poland
by Amazon Fulfillment
Poland Sp. z o.o., Wrocław